A
TWIST
OF THE
TONGUE

A
TWIST
OF THE
TONGUE

Insights and stories about the power of words
based on the Parshah of the Week

בראשית

BERAISHIS

Menachem Moshe Oppen

M'chon Harbotzas Torah, Inc.
3908 Bancroft Road • Baltimore, MD. 21-215
(301) 358-2543

CIS

C.I.S. Distributors
674 Eighth Street • Lakewood, N.J. 08701
(201) 367-7858 • (201) 364-1629

Published by C.I.S. Publications
a division of C.I.S. Communications, Inc.
674 Eighth Street, Lakewood, New Jersey 08701
(201) 367-7858/364-1629

Published in conjunction with
M'chon Harbotzas Torah
3908 Bancroft Road, Baltimore, Maryland 21215
(301) 358-2543

ISBN 0-935063-31-5 h/c
ISBN 0-935063-32-3 s/c

Jacket and Book Design by Ronda Kruger Green
Cover Illustration by Fruma Stern
Typography by Chaya Hoberman and Shami Reinman

Printed by Gross Bros., Union City, New Jersey, U.S.A.

TABLE OF CONTENTS

INTRODUCTION

Shlomo Hamelech teaches us in *Mishlei* (22:6), "Train a child in the way he should go, and even when he is old, he will not depart from it." At each stage of life, the child must learn according to his level of understanding.

From an early age, a child must be taught not to speak *loshon hora*. Even when the harm he causes others may be minimal, the harm to himself is enormous; he develops a pattern of behavior and an insensitivity to *loshon hora* that are difficult to combat as he gets older. Rabbi Simcha Zissel Ziv once compared such a person to a grown man, strong and capable in all ways, except that one hand remained the same as when he was a child. This describes any adult who develops physically but keeps his childish concepts and values.

Loshon hora can and does cause serious damage. Marriages have been destroyed. Victims have left a Torah environment because of lack of friends. Teachers' reputations have been ruined, resulting in loss of jobs and hardships to their families, not to mention handicapping their ability to teach Torah. Indeed, the misery caused to its victims is severe and long lasting.

The thoughtful adolescent can handle the problem of *loshon hora* in a mature way, analyzing what causes him to speak *loshon hora*, when he is most tempted to speak and how he can avoid stumbling into the traps laid by the *yetzer hora*.

Refraining from speaking *loshon hora*, on the other hand, brings many benefits. A person who restrains himself from harming others develops a sweet, pleasant personality, and his life becomes more enjoyable in general. He learns to bear life's inevitable frustrations with equanimity and remains calm in all situations. Dovid Hamelech set this as a goal when he said (*Tehillim* 34:13), "Who is the man that wants to live and have pleasure from his life? Guard your tongue from evil and your lips from speaking guilefully." If we want this level of pleasure for our children, we must begin early and continue long enough to incline them in the way they should go.

The Torah warns us to beware of speaking *loshon hora*. Many *mitzvos* are aimed at its prevention. The Chafetz Chaim wrote several volumes, compiling the *mitzvos* and commenting on them, warning us to guard our speech. Why? Why do we need to be told so much and so often to avoid *loshon hora*? Let's look at *loshon hora*, what it is, who is guilty of it, what it causes and how to avoid it.

Loshon hora is any communication, verbal or physical, that can cause harm or even discomfort to another person. Truth is not a defense when it comes to *loshon hora*; *loshon hora* can be true and the speaker guilty.

Obviously, people who are commanded to love their brothers as themselves have no right to cause pain to others. So why does anyone speak *loshon hora*? The main reason is probably that we speak without thinking. Someone once said, "Be sure to engage your brain before putting your mouth into gear." Most people do not want to hurt others but open their mouths carelessly.

Sometimes people engage in *loshon hora* because they

want to make themselves look important by revealing information that no one else has. These people may, in the backs of their minds, realize they should not be talking, but they can't resist the attention their friends are giving them.

Infrequently, some people may say bad things about those with whom they are angry. Not only are they guilty of *loshon hora*, but they are also guilty of violating the prohibition against taking revenge.

Loshon hora can cause great trouble in the world. The Chafetz Chaim said that *loshon hora* is more powerful than a sword; a sword can strike only those within an arm's length, but *loshon hora* can injure a person on the other side of the world. Reputations can be damaged, marriages destroyed, friendships broken, businesses bankrupted, all because of careless speech.

So what can we do to avoid this great evil? Probably, the best thing is to be aware of the great harm we can so easily cause. The purpose of this book is to heighten our awareness by providing a story related to *loshon hora* for each *Shabbos* so that we can remind ourselves weekly and reinforce our resolve to avoid *loshon hora*.

The stories recorded here did happen or could have happened. Where the stories are based on fact, although they may have happened a long time ago, names and many details were changed to avoid identifying the people involved.

We present these stories with the hope that they will help eliminate the real and ever-present danger of *loshon hora*. Sources of each story are listed at the end of the book. Many stories were heard from reliable sources and are so indicated without documented sources.

Although this book is basically a collection of stories, it is also a product of the efforts of many dedicated people. First and foremost, I am most grateful to my wife Leah for her encouragement and patience, as well as for typing the original manuscript. I would also like to express my profound appreciation to Mrs. Joseph Nelkin who devoted much time and toil to this book. I am thankful that she included editing this book among her numerous *chessed* projects. I am also deeply indebted to Rabbi Yosef Ashkenazi who has greatly enhanced this book with his skillful pen and exceptional talents. May he be successful in all his endeavors.

A special note of thanks is also due to the editorial and graphics departments of C.I.S. Communications Inc. of Lakewood, New Jersey. The product reflects their superior talents.

In closing, I would like to express my sincere and humble gratitude to the *Ribono Shel Olam* for granting me the privilege of bringing this book to the reading public. May it be His Will that this book bring benefit to its readers and honor to His Name.

> **The stories in this book were taken from reliable sources. Names of individuals and details that might have led to *Loshon Hora* were changed.**

בראשית

BERAISHIS

🌿🌿🌿🌿

The Power of Persuasion

The Chafetz Chaim points out that the first sin ever committed was a result of *loshon hora*. The serpent spoke *loshon hora* when he told Chava that Hashem was deceiving her when He said He would punish her if she ate from the Tree of Knowledge. The serpent claimed Hashem had threatened them with death for a selfish reason. He claimed Hashem did not want people to become as wise as He, for then people would also be able to create worlds.

The serpent was cursed because of this. He became the object of scorn, just as the talebearer eventually becomes despised by those who are aware of his evil tongue. Moreover, the serpent was no longer able to enjoy the taste of food, and he lost his ability to speak.

The talebearer will be punished in the same way. He will lose his ability to speak in the World to Come, and his source of livelihood will be diminished in this world. [1]

The Chafetz Chaim concludes that many people seek ways to be successful in business. In truth, there can be no greater guarantee to a substantial livelihood than to be careful not to speak *loshon hora*.[2]

From the following story we can see the great misfortune brought about by this sin:[3]

At the age of sixteen, Rav Yusha Ber Soloveitchik, the renowned Torah scholar with whom the dynasty of Brisk originated, was invited to the city of Minsk to give *shiurim* (*Talmudic* discourses). His *shiurim* were very popular, and he attracted many new students.

A very rich woman whom we will call Mrs. Kagan (not her real name), a descendant from very prestigious Torah scholars, suggested to her husband that Rav Yusha Ber would make an excellent match for their daughter.

Her husband, an extremely wealthy businessman, was not well learned, but he was scrupulous. Raised among *Chassidim*, he observed even the smallest *Chassidic* custom. Upon hearing her suggestion, her husband traveled to Minsk to personally observe Rav Yusha Ber and was very impressed with him.

While in Minsk, Mr. Kagan learned that Rav Yusha Ber would only accept a marriage proposal suggested by his father. Mr. Kagan went to his friend Rav Baruch Mordechai, the Bobroisker Rav, and asked him to write a letter to Rav Yusha Ber's father, the Kovner Rav, proposing the match. Mr. Kagan would guarantee the support of the new couple so that Rav Yusha Ber could continue learning uninterrupted.

Rabbi Baruch Mordechai consented and wrote the letter. He soon received an answer from the Kovner Rav saying that he intended to be in Minsk shortly and would discuss it with his son Rav Yusha Ber. Shortly thereafter, the match was arranged, and a day for the wedding was set.

The wedding, in honor of these two very prestigious families, was extraordinary. In honor of the Kovner Rav, great Torah scholars, presumably *Misnagdim*, came to the wedding, and in honor of the *Kallah's* side, prestigious *Chassidic* scholars came, all in perfect harmony, exchanging Torah thoughts and dancing together.

After the wedding, Rav Yusha Ber was given a house and all the *sefarim* he needed.

Some time later, he and his wife Rachel were blessed with a daughter. As more people heard his superb explanations of the *Gemara*, his reputation grew. Only Rachel's brother Aharon was unhappy that Rav Yusha Ber had entered the family, since Rav Yusha Ber had captured all the attention. When Aharon noticed that Rav Yusha Ber was not keeping certain *Chassidic* customs he complained to his father.

Aharon often complained to his father about the mistake of choosing Rav Yusha Ber as a son-in-law, claiming that Rav Yusha Ber was not the great scholar Mr. Kagan thought him to be. "He is very charismatic with people," Aharon said. "When people tell him their Torah explanations he compliments them and they are flattered. On the outside, he seems pious, but he is really lax and does not observe even simple customs."

At first, when Aharon spoke like this, his father replied, "You're just jealous." But as time went on, Aharon's words began to penetrate, and his father became more apprehensive.

After a few years, the evil outcome of Aharon's slander was apparent. The first day of *Sukkos* that year fell on a

Shabbos. Rav Yusha Ber sat at the right of his wealthy father-in-law in the front of the big *shul* on the bench reserved for the scholarly or wealthy.

"Now that it is *Shabbos* we must switch the order in which the *Payit* (special holiday services) is said. Which order should we switch to?" someone asked Rav Yusha Ber.

Rav Yusha Ber was unaccustomed to saying *Payit* at all, as it was not his father's custom to include them in the regular *Yom Tov* prayers. He admitted he did not know the order in which the *Payit* was to be recited.

Upon hearing this, Mr. Kagan thought to himself that his son was right. "Rav Yusha Ber is supposed to be a scholar and yet he does not even know the order of the *Payit*. He fooled me, and I'll never forgive him for this," thought the father-in-law. "I'll demand he divorce my precious daughter Rachel. I won't stand for this."

He kept his thoughts to himself until after *Simchas Torah*, and then, he confided the plan to his wife. Although she cried and pleaded with him not to carry it out, he would not budge. He even blamed her, because the match had been her idea in the first place.

Then, he went to his daughter and convinced her it would not be advantageous to stay married to this deceiver. He would no longer support them, and such a husband could bring no means of support. Eighteen-year-old Rochel was convinced.

Mr. Kagan finally approached Rav Yusha Ber. He interrupted Rav Yusha Ber as he was learning in his room. Without any explanation, Mr. Kagan exclaimed that his daughter wanted a divorce and that he was willing to give all the money Rav Yusha Ber would request if only he would consent to give the divorce.

Rav Yusha Ber realized it was not his wife's idea and attempted to convince his father-in-law that it was a great sin to break up a family, especially with a small child. Finally, Rav Yusha Ber threatened to take his wife and child and live on his own. He would not divorce his wife without cause.

However, when he told his wife of his plan to leave, to his surprise and disbelief, he found that her father had already convinced her, and he could not change her mind. Having no alternative he was forced to give her the divorce. Rav Yusha Ber not only refused any money as compensation but left everything his father-in-law had ever given him, including *sefarim* and clothing.

After the divorce procedure, Rav Yusha Ber put on his old suit, already small, took only his belongings and *sefarim* from before the marriage and was about to leave. His mother-in-law, the only one in the family who sided with him, came in crying. Rav Yusha Ber asked her for forgiveness for perhaps not having given her the proper respect during the years he had stayed in her house. He begged her to take good care of her grandchild and kissed his little daughter good-bye.

Rav Yusha Ber eventually remarried and had a son who illuminated the whole world with his Torah, Rav Chaim Soloveitchik, the famous Rav of Brisk. But the scars from this tragic chapter in his early years were never completely healed.

נח

NOACH

❧❧❧❧

Bearing Responsibility for the Outcome

History has proven again and again that only evil results from speaking *loshon hora*. In *Parshas Noach*, we see the calamity which befell Chom. Instead of covering his drunken father, Chom belittled him by going outside and revealing Noach's shameful situation to his brothers. As a result of disgracing his father, Chom's family was accursed to be slaves throughout the generations.

The *Gemara* states that the people in the western part of Eretz Yisrael referred to *loshon hora* as the triple tongue. This is because *loshon hora* causes death to three people: the one who speaks it, the one who accepts it and the one about whom it is spoken.[4]

Rashi explains that the one who accepts the evil tale may be provoked to fight the subject of the *loshon hora*. This fight may lead to both of their deaths. An angry relative may then kill the speaker who was the actual cause of the death. Although the speaker did not intend such a terrible outcome to result, he is still held responsible. The following examples from the Torah highlight this point:

Towards the end of *Parshas Noach*, the Torah records the death of Charan, the brother of Avram. It states that Charan died before Terach. *Rashi*₅ states that Terach is held responsible for his son Charan's death; for when Terach told Nimrod that Avram had destroyed idols, Nimrod had Avram thrown into a burning furnace.

Charan was asked with whom he sided, Avram or Nimrod.

"If Avram lives, I'm on his side," Charan replied. "If he dies, I'm on Nimrod's side."

When Avram lived, Nimrod threw Charan into the furnace. Charan, who was not worthy of a miracle, died.

Although Terach had no intention of causing Charan's death, it is attributed to him because it was a consequence of his *loshon hora* when he told Nimrod that Avram had destroyed idols. Any words that can be harmful to someone, even in a roundabout way, are considered *loshon hora*.₆

The *Gemara*₇ relates the story of the tragic death of Rav Ada. At the time of the incident, it was the custom that when a *Talmid Chacham* entered a city to sell goods, he was extended certain courtesies to hasten the sale and enable him to return quickly to his studies. These privileges were extended only to scholars.

One day, Rav Dimi arrived with a shipload of figs. Rav Ada was sent to test him to see if he was worthy of a scholar's privileges. Rav Ada asked him a difficult question which he could not answer. Consequently, Rav Dimi was denied the privileges and his figs spoiled before he could sell them.

Rav Dimi complained to Rav Yosef that it was not fair that

he should be denied privileges just because he did not know the answer to a difficult question. Rav Yosef said that if Rav Ada went about the test in an unjust way, he deserved to be punished. Shortly afterwards, Rav Ada passed away.

Rav Yosef bemoaned the fact that he might have been the cause of Rav Ada's death, that his words had served as a curse. Rav Dimi also felt responsible, because had he disregarded the matter, Rav Ada would not have died.

Rava said, "It is I who am responsible, for I hadn't completely forgiven Rav Ada for the times when he did not show the proper respect to my messengers. Had I done so, he would not have been punished."

Abaye said, "I am to blame. Rav Ada felt that my lectures were inferior to those of Rava, and I did not completely forgive him when he expressed these feelings to others."

Rav Nachum said, "I am at fault, because when Rav Ada did not come on time to help me prepare for my lecture, I said, 'If Rav Ada is not here, he must have died.' This expression may have been the cause of his death."

Tosefos cites the *Gemara* in *Shabbos*[8] which states that a person responsible for someone else's punishment cannot enter Hashem's inner sphere in Gan Eden. Each scholar felt he was responsible and must do *teshuvah* for being even a remote cause of Rav Ada's misfortune.

I n the *Gemara Sanhedrin*[9] we find that Dovid Hamelech suffered severely because of the *loshon hora* he had unwittingly caused.

When Dovid was running from Shaul, he had not eaten for many days. Finally, he reached the city of Nov. There, he pretended he was carrying out a secret mission for Shaul and asked Achimelech, the *Kohain Gadol*, for food and a sword. Unaware that Dovid was running from Shaul, Achimelech complied. Neither Achimelech nor Dovid was aware that they were being watched by Do'eg. Do'eg then returned and informed Shaul that Achimelech was guilty of treason.

Do'eg was guilty of *loshon hora* in relating the incident to Shaul, since he gave the impression that Achimelech took part in a conspiracy against the king. Shaul ordered that not only Achimelech be put to death but that the whole city of Nov be wiped out as a lesson for all conspirators.

Shaul was subsequently punished in that he and his sons were killed in battle. Do'eg was punished for his *loshon hora* by premature death, and he also lost his portion in the World to Come.

Dovid also suffered.

The *Gemara* relates that Hashem said to Dovid, "On account of you, the city of Nov was destroyed, Do'eg lost his portion in the World to Come and Shaul and his three sons were killed. This sin can be expiated in one of two ways. Either your children will be killed, or you will be handed over to your enemies."

Dovid replied that he would rather be handed over to his enemies than have calamity befall his children. As a result of this choice, Dovid was captured one *Erev Shabbos* as he was going to the city of Schor Heza. Satan appeared in the guise of a deer. Dovid pursued the deer all the way to the land of the Plishtim. This was a dangerous place for Dovid, because a few years before, Dovid had killed Golyas, the Plishti giant, thereby disgracing the entire nation of the Plishtim.

Golyas' brother Yishbi recognized Dovid as the one who

had killed his brother. Yishbi seized this opportunity for revenge. He captured Dovid and tied him under the heavy beams of an olive press so that it would slowly bear down on top of Dovid. However, a miracle occurred, and the ground under Dovid sank down. The heavy beams landed on the ground, while Dovid lay beneath the surface unharmed.

In the meantime, Dovid's general Avishai was preparing for *Shabbos*. As he washed his hair, he noticed drops of blood in the water. Also, a dove alighted beside him and died. He realized he was being given a sign that there was danger to *Bnai Yisrael*, He went to Dovid's house, but was unable to find him. He took Dovid's personal mule, hoping it would lead him to Dovid. Avishai followed it straight to the land of Plishtim.

There, Avishai saw the mother of Golyas spinning thread. When the handle of her spinning wheel fell off, she asked Avishai to fetch it. He picked it up and threw it at her, killing her.

When Yishbi saw Dovid's general, he decided to kill Dovid quickly. He pulled Dovid from under the press, threw him into the air and placed a spear beneath him, hoping he would fall upon the spear and die. Avishai uttered one of the Names of Hashem, and Dovid remained suspended in midair, far above the poised spear.

Avishai asked Dovid how he had been captured. Dovid told him he was being punished for what had happened to Nov and that he had chosen to be captured rather than have his children killed. Avishai suggested to Dovid that his choice was unwise and that he should pray to Hashem to be saved.

Dovid asked Avishai to pray with him, and their prayers

were answered. Again, Avishai uttered the Name of Hashem, and Dovid descended to the ground. Together, they pursued Yishbi and overcame him. But since Dovid was saved, he had yet to atone for the *loshon hora*. Unfortunately, this was only accomplished after Dovid's children were almost entirely wiped out.

From the above stories we learn how careful one must be not to cause suffering to another person. Understanding this can give us the proper insight to the following story: [10]

As Rav of Slutzk, Rav Yushe Ber Soloveitchik was asked to settle many disputes. Though he always tried to be fair, he found it impossible to please everyone in every decision.

One hot summer day, when the Rav of Slutzk was learning with his son Chaim (later known as Rav Chaim Brisker), a butcher entered the room and started to scream at the Rav. The butcher accused the Rav of judging him unfairly.

"Yesterday, I was right in my dispute," the butcher shouted. "I lost because the other party had bribed you."

The Rav stood quietly listening to all of the butcher's shouts, complaints and insults. The intruder started to leave with clenched fists.

"I forgive you," said the Rav as he escorted the man from the room. "I realize it is very painful for you to suffer the monetary loss involved in this dispute. In time of distress, you cannot be held responsible for your actions."

The next day, as the butcher was bringing home some cows he had bought, they stampeded and killed him.

When the Rav heard of it, he asked his son Reb Chaim

several times, "Do you think I could have been responsible for his death?" This thought was so disturbing that he trembled as he spoke.

"How could you possibly be responsible?" his son Chaim replied. "You forgave him."

"How do you know I forgave him?" asked Rav Yushe Ber.

"I heard you say so as he was leaving," Chaim answered him.

Only after much reassurance did the Rav compose himself. He not only attended the funeral but personally escorted the deceased to the distant graveyard. He cried and prayed over his grave. He recited *Kaddish* for his sake the whole year, and learned *Mishanyos* every day in his merit. And for the rest of his life, the Rav acted as one would on the *Yahrzeit* of his own parents. He fasted, said *Kaddish* and learned *Mishanyos* for the soul of the deceased.

Near the end of this *Parshah*, the Torah mentions the death of Terach. *Rashi*[11] explains that he actually died over sixty years after his son Avram left him. However, the Torah mentions Terach's death out of sequence, before the departure of Avram to the land of Canaan. This is to avoid the impression that Avram did not respect his aging father, deserting him in his old age.

Though the essence of Torah is truth, it gave the impression that Terach had died over sixty years earlier. The order of events was deliberately changed so that no one would defame Avram who did not leave voluntarily but was expressly commanded by Hashem to leave his father. This lesson teaches us to be extremely cautious about impressions we give concerning others.

לך לך

LECH LECHO

❧❧❧❧

The Consequences of Expression

The power of speech is illustrated in various ways throughout this *Parshah*. When Hagar became pregnant immediately after marrying Avraham, she considered this proof that Sarah was not the *tzadekes* she seemed to be. Otherwise, Hagar reasoned, Sarah would also have had children from Avraham during their long marriage.

Had Hagar kept her thoughts to herself, she would not have suffered as she did. However, when she disgraced Sarah verbally in front of Avraham, grave consequences followed.

Sarah went to Avraham and said,₁₂ "I must reproach you, for you hear me being disgraced and remain silent."

Avraham reacted by allowing Sarah to deal with Hagar so harshly that it resulted in the miscarriage of Hagar's first child.

From the following incident we can learn not only the evil outcome of derogatory speech but also the great reward for refraining from it. When Sarah went down to

Egypt, she was asked by Pharaoh's servants about her relationship to Avraham. She replied that she was his sister. Although Lot was aware that she was Avraham's wife, he did not reveal this, thus protecting Avraham's life. Had Avraham died, Lot would have been the closest surviving relative, and he would have received gifts just as Avraham had when he was thought to be Sarah's closest relative. However, Lot restrained himself, and he was rewarded by Hashem with the gift of two nations, Amon and Moav.

Lot merited to be treated as a son of Avraham. As *Rashi*[13] states, the lands of Amon and Moav were originally intended for Avraham. However, since Lot remained silent, he was rewarded with the status of a son, thus inheriting these two countries from Avraham. *Rashi*[14] also states that in this merit he was saved when the city of Sedom was destroyed.

Another illustration of the great reward for restraint from speaking evil can be seen from the following story about one of the greatest *Talmidei Chachamim* of the last generation:[15]

The *Sefer Sdei Chemed* has become a classic. There is hardly a *Yeshivah* without one. It discusses almost every topic in encyclopedic detail. It gives thousands of references, even on topics mentioned by the author incidentally. Anyone who reads this *sefer* cannot help but marvel at the genius of its author Rav Chaim Chizkiyahu Medini.

Rav Chaim Chizkiyahu Medini, the Rav of Chevron, was very sick at the end of his life. At this time, he revealed to his disciples the secret of his extraordinary gift.

In his youth, when he had lived in Egypt, a wise and wealthy man named Mr. Zerich opened a *Yeshivah* and

Kollel for young married students. Rav Chaim Chizkiyahu, newly married, joined this *Kollel*. He was successful in his studies and had a friendly disposition which made him very popular.

He was constantly surrounded with other students who needed questions answered or who sought deeper insights into their studies. Although Rav Chaim Chizkiyahu was an extremely good student, his capabilities were not exceptional. He was gracious with the knowledge he acquired after many hours of diligent study.

Among the students in this *Kollel* was a very wealthy boy named Yosef Deptha who had been living in Egypt for just a few years. This youth had unfortunately suffered from mental problems, a fact which wasn't known to the people of Egypt. He appeared to be a respectable and sincere student.

Yosef became very jealous of Rav Chaim Chizkiyahu, because everyone else did not befriend him as they befriended Rav Chaim. If he could only get rid of Rav Chaim! Even if Yosef wouldn't be befriended as much as he would like to be, at least he wouldn't have to see someone else being befriended. He must see to it that Rav Chaim leave the *Kollel*, or he wouldn't be able to soothe his aching heart. He could no longer concentrate on his studies, and at last, his disturbed mind found a solution to the problem.

That evening, he contacted one of the maids who worked for Mr. Zerich. He offered her a large sum of money if she would make Rav Chaim appear to be a wicked person who commits grave sins. The money meant a lot to her, and she consented. To be sure his plan would work, Yosef spent much time explaining to her exactly what she was to do.

The next day, she came running into the *Bais Medrash*,

29

disturbing everyone's studies. She ran over to Rav Chaim and screamed, "You claim to be a holy man, but you are far from it. A holy man would not torture an innocent lady." She then spat at him and ran out.

This was just what Yosef needed.

"Did you hear that?" Yosef started to protest. "How can we leave such a student in the *Yeshivah*? He will bring disgrace to the Torah."

Yosef continued to convince the students that although it would be a loss to the *Yeshivah* if Rav Chaim left, it would be worse if he remained. Soon, a delegation of many boys agreed to ask Mr. Zerich to expel Chaim from the *Yeshivah*.

When the delegation approached Mr. Zerich's house, his wife answered the door. She informed them that Mr. Zerich had left town and would not return for two weeks. They told her that the situation was desperate and that since her husband was not home, she should act in his stead and have Rav Chaim expelled.

She replied that she had nothing to do with running the *Yeshivah*. They had no choice but to wait.

During these two weeks, the wealthy boy Yosef suddenly died. During the eulogy, although not much was known about him, the fact that he took his studies seriously and showed a deep concern for the welfare for the *Yeshivah* was constantly repeated.

When Mr. Zerich finally returned, the delegation felt obligated to continue what their departed friend Yosef had started. They approached Mr. Zerich and demanded that Rav Chaim be expelled. They expressed regret that Yosef was no longer with them, but they conveyed his feelings. The students explained why it would be detrimental to the

Yeshivah if Rav Chaim should remain.

Mr. Zerich carefully took all the facts into consideration, and told the delegation that he would have to review the matter before arriving at a decision. Mr. Zerich, who was a very wise person and an expert in human nature, went directly to the *Bais Medrash*.

He observed Rav Chaim as he was learning. Mr. Zerich sat and watched for a half hour without taking his eyes off of Rav Chaim.

Finally, he gave a bang on the table and announced, "Everyone should know that whatever was said about Rav Chaim is all a bluff, and I do not want to hear another word concerning this."

He went home and fired his maid in disgust.

Although Rav Chaim stayed in the *Yeshivah*, he quickly lost popularity. Students didn't approach him any more. Even his learning partners were regarded with disdain, and soon, he learned only by himself for most of the day.

As time went on, Mr. Zerich's maid ran out of money. She could not find employment, and the money Yosef had given her dwindled away. One day, she approached Rav Chaim on his way to the *Yeshivah* and asked him to speak to Mr. Zerich on her behalf. She offered to announce the truth publicly and confess that she was hired by Yosef as a result of his jealousy.

When Rav Chaim heard this, he felt relieved. At last, he had an opportunity to clear his name and erase the misconceptions about him. Once again, he would be able to live normally.

However, on second thought, he felt it would be a tremendous *Chillul Hashem* if people were to learn how underhanded Yosef had really been. This would cast a bad light on all those in Mr. Zerich's *Yeshivah*. Rather than reopen the issue, Rav Chaim decided to sacrifice his name for the benefit of the *Yeshivah*. He told the maid he would find her a job, with Mr. Zerich or with someone else, on the condition that she never reveal to anyone what really happened. She readily consented.

After that, Rav Chaim Chizkiyahu Medini concluded, whenever he opened any *sefer*, he felt as he had never felt before. He quickly comprehended everything, and nothing was forgotten.

VAYAIRO

Some Laws To Be Learned

Many laws and lessons concerning *loshon hora* can be understood from this *Parshah*. We find that Hashem misquotes Sarah as saying "I am old" when she had actually said Avraham was old. Since Avraham could object to being called "old," Hashem misquoted Sarah.[16]

The Chafetz Chaim[17] derived an important *Halachah* from this. Although there is nothing wrong with being old, if someone objects to being referred to as old, it is forbidden to mention it, for doing so may arouse his ill feelings against the speaker. One certainly may not tell someone that someone else referred to him as fat or stupid, etc. This is included in the prohibition of *rechilus*. The Chafetz Chaim writes[18] that if one has no choice, it is better to lie than to speak *rechilus*.

In addition, the Chafetz Chaim[19] writes that at times one may speak *loshon hora* if doing so will protect someone from a bad influence. In this *Parshah*, we find that the people of Sedom are always mentioned with degradation.

33

Lot made a grave mistake when he decided to dwell in Sedom. The *malachim*[20] who came to save him spent the night with Lot discussing the people of Sedom, proving their evilness and announcing the imminent destruction of their city. This was done to show Lot his error and served as a warning not to dwell amongst *reshaim* in the future.

Another important rule which the Chafetz Chaim[21] highlights is that even when *loshon hora* is permitted (as for a beneficial purpose), one may not exaggerate. Exaggeration is a common cause of misunderstanding and error. Therefore, even when one hears beneficial information one must be wary of exaggeration. Perhaps all the facts have not been related. Investigate thoroughly prior to taking any action.

Hashem said to Avraham that He had heard many complaints and cries coming from the tortured victims of Sedom. However, Hashem said, perhaps they are exaggerating the situation.[22] Only if the complaints were accurate would Sedom be destroyed. Whenever one hears complaints, one must investigate and be wary of exaggeration before taking action.

One is not only discouraged from exaggerating but also from adding derogatory details if they serve no purpose.[23]

❧❧❧❧

Payment for Politeness

Both daughters of Lot had children from their father. The oldest daughter called her child Moav, meaning "from the

34

father." This brought unnecessary disgrace to Lot. The younger daughter called her son Amon, meaning "from my nation," which did not reveal the exact origin of the child. For this, she received a great reward. Her descendants were not only protected from a major attack by the *Bnai Yisrael* while they were on their way to Eretz Yisrael, but in addition, they were not afflicted by border disputes nor disturbed in any manner.[24]

The following story about the Chafetz Chaim also illustrates the importance of politeness:[25]

The Chafetz Chaim was once traveling with another *Talmid Chacham*. As they passed through a city, they interrupted their journey and found a Jewish home in which to eat and sleep overnight. The owner of the house was thrilled to have such esteemed guests. He told his wife to serve only the very best food.

As they were eating, the host asked his guests if they were enjoying the meal. The Chafetz Chaim complimented the host. The other guest also complimented the fine food but mentioned that the soup was lacking some salt. The host immediately brought salt.

"Now it's perfect," he said.

While the host was in the kitchen, the Chafetz Chaim said to his companion harshly, "What have you done? My whole life I have been careful not to hear any *loshon hora*. Now you have spoken *loshon hora*."

"I haven't mentioned a soul," the companion replied. "How could I have possibly spoken *loshon hora*?"

"I'm referring to the soup," the Chafetz Chaim said sternly. "Who do you think cooks the soup? It is probably a poor widow. For all you know, she could lose her job because of your complaint."

"Maybe I shouldn't have said it, but I'm sure that no harm was done."

"Let us go to the kitchen and see," the Chafetz Chaim suggested.

As they approached the kitchen, they heard sobs.

"The Rabbi complained that there was no salt in the soup," the hostess was saying. "How could you make such a stupid mistake?"

"I remember distinctly that I put salt in the soup," the cook replied.

"Why do you lie to me?" insisted the hostess. "The Rabbi says there is no salt in the soup, and you have the nerve to say there is!?"

The host tried to calm his wife down, but it only made matters worse. His wife had already become furious and suggested the cook be fired.

Hearing this, the Chafetz Chaim's companion ran into the kitchen. His presence brought immediate silence. He sincerely apologized to the cook for causing her such distress and praised the rest of the meal so much that he convinced the hostess it would be a great loss to replace such a fine cook. He did not leave until he was finally sure there were no ill feelings.

Then he admitted to the Chafetz Chaim that, although it had seemed very far-fetched, seeing was believing. He would be more careful in the future.

חיי שרה

CHAYAI SARAH

❧❧❧❧

He Remembers the Sins of the Fathers

In this *Parshah*, we find the story of a great man who sought tremendous spiritual treasures but was unsuccessful. As in most cases, this misfortune is also related to *loshon hora*.

Avraham's greatest disciple, Eliezer, was not only extremely intelligent and learned but also an excellent teacher. He knew how to transmit the deep teachings of Avraham to others. He was a holy man and a great *tzaddik*, a devoted disciple whom Avraham considered a worthy successor should he have no children.

When it was time for Yitzchak to wed, Avraham sent his reliable disciple Eliezer to the distant land of Charan to find a suitable mate for his son. However, Eliezer had a daughter whom he had righteously raised, and he suggested to Avraham that she become Yitzchak's wife.

Avraham rejected this proposal. He told Eliezer that he should not consider his daughter a suitable match for Yitzchak. Although Eliezer's daughter may very well have been a *tzadekes*, since Eliezer was descended from Canaan, the son of Chom, their families could not intermarry. [26]

The reason for this had occurred ten generations earlier when Noach had blessed Shem, the ancestor of Avraham, and cursed Chom, the ancestor of Eliezer. Those who are cursed cannot marry those who are blessed. This was distressing to Eliezer who had hoped that the chosen people would descend from him.

The cause of this curse is stated clearly in the Torah. [27] When Chom became aware that Noach acted improperly after becoming drunk, he went out and broadcast it to his brothers, who immediately corrected the situation. Had Chom corrected the situation himself and not disgraced his father, his descendant Eliezer might not have suffered such an eternal loss.

༒༒༒༒

Juicy Loshon Hora

It is extremely important that we be aware of the great harm caused by *loshon hora*. Even pinpointing a few minor things can be catastrophic. Aside from the fact that it is an *aveirah* to speak *loshon hora*, whether or not we can comprehend why, history has often shown that one thing leads to another. Sometimes the unfortunate results become apparent only many years later.

Small details can often be the deciding factor in keeping a job or marrying a particular person. The *yetzer hora* can easily persuade us to speak *loshon hora* if we don't earnestly fear the potential harm we could wreak.

This can be illustrated by the explanation given by Rav Simchah Zissel Ziv to the following *Gemara*[28] which states that Rav Meir was the author of three hundred different parables concerning foxes, including the following example:

There was once a small fox wandering in the forest. Suddenly, he was approached by a fierce, hungry lion. The fox realized his life was in danger and quickly said to the lion, "Don't make a silly mistake. If you devour a skinny fox like me, you'll never satisfy your hunger. If you spare my life, I will show you a very heavy man. He is so fleshy that you can fill yourself up and have plenty to spare."

The lion followed the fox through the thickets until they saw an overweight man. He was a Jewish hunter who made his living trapping animals. He stood next to his concealed trap with a *Tehillim* in his hands, praying that he be spared from danger and that he be successful in his endeavors.

He truly looked luscious to the lion, but the lion hesitated.

"I am afraid that I will be punished if I attack a man who is praying," the lion said to the fox.

"Don't worry," said the fox. "The wicked are not punished immediately. The punishment will bring suffering only to your children or grandchildren. You can enjoy yourself."

The lion then leaped towards his tasty meal. But lo and behold, he landed right on a grass-concealed trap, next to the hunter. He quickly fell into a deep pit.

The fox knew he was safe and peered into the pit.

"Didn't you tell me that no evil would befall me?" the angry lion called up. "Didn't you say only my children would suffer?"

"Of course," replied the fox. "You were not punished for attempting to eat this man. You are suffering for the man your father ate."

"What lesson did Rabbi Meir want to teach us with this parable?" asks Rav Simchah Zissel Ziv. "Why didn't the lion think of the possibility that the man was a hunter with a trap? Or of the possibility that he would suffer for his father's sins? Obviously, his temptation dulled his mind."

One who enjoys speaking *loshon hora* is in the greatest danger. Without true fear, the *yetzer hora* is apt to fool and persuade him that any given situation is different, permissible or even a *mitzvah*. Especially when there might be a good purpose in speaking, temptation dulls the mind. Rather than stop and wonder if we are correct, we will justify ourselves with unjust excuses. However, if we realize how dreadful *loshon hora* is, we will lose our temptation to speak it, and we will follow our reason rather than our lusts.

The difference between one who has an inner desire to speak *loshon hora* but restrains himself only to follow the *Halachah* and one who is intelligent enough not to even want to speak can be explained with the following parable: 29

Many years ago in Europe, the Jews were forced to work and live on farms owned by wealthy gentiles. In one village, there lived a cruel *poretz* who showed no respect towards his Jewish servants.

One day, a friend of his told him, "You know what your servants think of you? They hate you so much that if you would even touch some delicious wine, they would refuse to drink it!"

This made the *poretz* furious. He immediately ordered one of his Jewish farmers to be brought to him.

"Is it true that if I touch this wine, you won't drink it?" he asked.

"Yes," was the reply.

"So, you hate me!" he shouted.

"No, no," replied the farmer. "According to Jewish law we are forbidden to drink wine touched by a gentile, but not because we hate you. If you touched water or juice, we would gladly drink it."

"Excuses, excuses. You hate me! I know it!"

The *poretz* ordered a large jug of wine and put his hands in.

"Drink!" he ordered.

"I am sorry, but the little I know about Jewish law, I must keep," said the farmer. "I refuse to drink no matter what you do."

Hearing this, the *poretz* had three of his strongest men come in. One twisted the farmer's right arm and the other the left. The third person poured the flask of wine down his throat.

The wine was strong and tasty, and the farmer became drunk and fell asleep on the ground.

When he awakened, the *poretz* asked him, "Now what do you have to say for yourself?"

"I would like to ask the *poretz* one small favor," the farmer replied. "The next time you force me to drink such delicious wine, can you have one man holding me and two men pouring?"

There are times when we must say certain things about others. The *Halachah* demands that certain facts be presented to avoid suffering and loss to the innocent. However, when we speak, we should do it as a duty to fulfill and not because we enjoy defaming other people. If one derives personal pleasure from defaming and belittling others, one may easily go beyond what he is required and allowed to do and, Heaven forbid, be guilty of *loshon hora*.

Aside from the immediate harm caused by *loshon hora*, we should also realize that the exile is prolonged because of *loshon hora* (as explained by the Chafetz Chaim[30]).

When *Mashiach* will come, we will all receive great honors. To be worthy of such honor we must be careful of the honor of others, and certainly not defame others with *loshon hora*. (Therefore, we find that a person who honors another by quoting Torah, etc., in his name, brings redemption to the world.)

The following story should reinforce our dislike for *loshon hora*.[31]

G ood help is hard to come by. This is true for both the employee and the employer. Each seeks his own satisfaction and benefit. While pondering these two points, Mr. Levinson came across a want ad in the newspaper. A competent bookkeeper with experience was looking for a job.

Mr. Levinson immediately dialed the telephone number listed in the advertisement because his knitting factory was in dire need of a competent bookkeeper. An honest, industrious worker was difficult to come by. Mr. Levinson needed someone reliable, familiar with large business accounting and able to work well alone.

A serious voice answered on the other end of the telephone. After inquiring whether this was the party interested in a job, Mr. Levinson arranged an interview for the following day.

Inwardly, Mr. Levinson was pleased with the serious tone of the voice on the telephone. He was optimistic. Mr. Jackman hung up the receiver with a good feeling too.

He knocked on Mr. Levinson's office door promptly at four o'clock the next afternoon. Mr. Levinson was very impressed with Mr. Jackman's answers to his questions and was ready to give him the job right then and there. Due to protocol, however, he told Mr. Jackson that a definite answer would have to wait for a few days and that he would let him know by telephone.

Yisrael Jackman left the Levinson Knitting Company in better spirits that when he had come. He had had a sad life and was looking forward to a nice change in the London atmosphere. As a boy, he had experienced the Nazi horrors. Naturally soft spoken, he became more withdrawn after the war. He didn't voice his opinions in public and strangers thought him an introvert. People found it strange that a middle-aged man wasn't opinionated. Others claimed that Mr. Jackman was so quiet because he was not intelligent enough to have ideas on different subjects. This led Mr. Jackman to move his family from Scotland to England. He thought that a change of place would do his family some good.

He had received Mr. Levinson's call about the job offer after two weeks of being in a rented apartment in one of London's poorer sections. Mrs. Jackman and their son Yossi were pleased with the outcome of the job interview. They understood that it was just a matter of time until Mr. Levinson would call back with an affirmative answer.

Yitzchak Levinson appreciated *Shabbos* for the rest it gave him from his business after each hectic week of work. *Motzai Shabbos* was his only opportunity to visit friends or have guests come to his home. He had planned to call Mr. Jackman to finalize his acceptance as head bookkeeper for the firm the *Motzai Shabbos* after the interview, but Mrs. Levinson reminded him that his sister Devora would arrive shortly to visit. There was no choice but to postpone the business call until after entertaining his sister and brother-in-law.

Close knit as the Levinson family was, Yitzchak thought his sister a little too voluble at times. Nevertheless, he was grateful that she had taken care of him after their mother had died and then later married him off.

Devora and her husband arrived on time, and Mrs. Levinson took them into the living room. As usual, conversation was no problem, especially with Devora. While sipping coffee, she inquired about her brother's business. Yitzchak was more than pleased to inform her of his luck at finding a suitable bookkeeper. Devora insisted on knowing more about his new employee and asked her brother for his name.

"Mr. Yisrael Jackman who's just moved from Scotland to London," he answered.

"You aren't serious!?" Devora exclaimed. "You aren't actually thinking of hiring him as a bookkeeper?"

Astonished at his sister's unexpected reaction, Mr. Levinson asked for one good reason why she found him incapable of handling the job.

"Yitzchak, you mean to tell me you'd be willing to accept an employee for such an important position without even inquiring about his references? Why, I knew the man during the time I lived in Scotland, and anyone who knows him would tell you the same. He's a very nice man who doesn't happen to be too intelligent. Perhaps he gives a serious impression at first, but it's probably nothing more than a cover for what he lacks inside."

Yitzchak Levinson was totally confused. How could he have misjudged a person so badly?

"Are you quite sure we're talking about the same person?" he asked.

"Quite," answered the sister, in a tone that told Yitzchak she knew what she was talking about.

Yitzchak explained to his sister that he was now in a predicament since it was almost definitely understood from their interview a few days earlier that Mr. Jackman would be accepted for the job. The planned telephone call was more protocol than anything else.

"Simply tell Mr. Jackman that your plans have changed unexpectedly, and his services aren't needed at the present time," she explained.

Difficult as it was, Mr. Levinson decided to take his sister's advice. His business was doing too well to risk entrusting an incompetent person with the books. Although his sister's visit had turned out less pleasant than expected, at least Yitzchak felt his sister had done his business a good turn by offering the information about Mr. Jackman.

While Mrs. Levinson was cleaning up after the guests, Mr. Levinson went into his study and called the Jackman household. He politely informed Mr. Jackson about the change and apologized for having put him to the trouble of coming down to the office for an interview.

Mr. Jackman found it hard to inform his family of the sad news. Mrs. Jackman had been so excited ever since her husband returned from the interview with Mr. Levinson; she had made all sorts of plans about what to do with her husband's first paycheck. Since they had moved to London, the household had been on a very strict budget until the head of the family would find work. It was difficult for Mr. Jackman to disappoint his wife and son so deeply. With no choice, he explained to them the reason for Mr. Levinson's telephone call.

Not wasting any time, Mr. Jackman immediately began job hunting again and started answering the advertisements in the paper. Every office had the same reaction. He would be given a definite answer in a matter of days. Meanwhile, each employer was interested in Mr. Jackman's references. Word spread quickly, and it became known that Mr. Levinson had considered hiring Mr. Jackman. It was only natural for anyone considering hiring the new London resident to call Mr. Levinson and ask him for his reason for not taking on Mr. Jackman.

That Monday morning, Mr. Levinson's telephone didn't stop ringing. Everyone was asking the same questions about Mr. Jackman. Yitzchak Levinson was finding it difficult to be vague, and under pressure from all his callers, he revealed what he knew about Yisrael Jackman.

By the end of the week, Mr. Jackman made the rounds at

all the offices he had been to earlier in the week. Extremely disappointed, he returned home with no chance of being hired in the near future. He was having no luck in London, and he began to wonder if he had made the right decision of moving his family from Scotland. Mrs. Jackman took the news much harder than did her husband. They had reached the bottom of their savings and had no money left, even for basics. Mrs. Jackman couldn't control herself and broke down crying. There wasn't much with which her husband could comfort her.

Shy as he was, Mr. Jackman had no choice at this point but to accept his friendly neighbor's offer to speak to someone about finding him a job. When this was also unsuccessful, Mr. Jackman shamefully accepted his neighbor's financial loan. Other neighbors anonymously donated some money for the staples necessary to the Jackman family. After a week, this money was also gone.

Winter had already arrived and the lack of proper food and warm clothing was very evident in the Jackman apartment. To make matters worse, job opportunities were non-existent at this point.

Mr. Jackman did not give up. Still inquiring about any available jobs, he received a tip on a possible opening at a factory just outside London. Although the distance was great, Mr. Jackman was willing to try anything. He left early the next morning in a snowstorm and didn't pay any attention to the weather or to his inadequate winter coat. He was too concerned with finding work.

After a long trip, Mr. Jackman reached his destination and was pleased with his interview. Mr. Lasky, who owned the factory, assured him that the bookkeeping job was his.

Things finally seemed to be going right.

As he was returning home, Mr. Jackman was so excited he didn't take notice how he was shivering and coughing. When he finally stepped into his apartment, it all began to catch up with him. Mrs. Jackman was pleased with the good news of work but very worried about her husband's health. She insisted on taking his temperature and was horrified to see the mercury register shockingly high. Mr. Jackman was complaining of piercing back pains that wouldn't let up. Mrs. Jackman phoned the doctor who came immediately. After a thorough examination, the doctor said that Mr. Jackman was suffering from a bad case of pneumonia and should be transferred to a hospital at once.

The next three days were agonizing for Mrs. Jackman and her son. Mr. Jackman lost consciousness, and the doctors were very worried. They were having trouble keeping the temperature down, and this was taking a heavy toll on the patient.

On the third day, the worst happened. Mr. Jackman died.

Tragedy had hit the Jackman household. The entire neighborhood was in shock when they heard the news. Mr. Jackman was never known to be sick. It had all happened so suddenly to such a young man with a wife and child.

Many people attended his funeral the following day, including businessmen from the community. Somehow, even Mr. Levinson felt obligated to go, as did the other men who had refused Mr. Jackman a job.

Mr. Farber, an active community member who was president of the local *shul*, delivered the eulogy. His words pierced the hearts of everyone present.

"The tragedy of Yisrael Jackman's untimely death is more

severe than we might think. I inquired from the family as to how he became ill and was astonished to hear the response. Because he was refused work within the county, Mr. Jackman had to go seek a job further afield. It was a cold wintry day, and he left the house poorly dressed. The result was a severe case of pneumonia. In trying to improve the living conditions of his family, Mr. Jackman has left behind a young widow and orphan.

"The questions remains. Who is to blame? All the reasons given for not hiring Yisrael Jackman were false rumors which had no foundation. As *Chazal* say: '*Loshon hora* is equivalent to murder,' and we have spoken and accepted *loshon hora* about Mr. Jackman. We all bear guilt for his death, as accusative as it may sound. I ask forgiveness from the deceased in the name of the entire community. We realize we have sinned. We ask to be forgiven."

Every businessman who had refused work to Mr. Jackman felt overcome with guilt. Yitzchak Levinson felt worse than all of them, as he blamed himself wholly for starting the rumor, and all because he believed what his sister Devora had told him. Knowing Devora, he should have realized it was no more than gossip. Why did he take her so seriously and let the situation get so far out of hand? Unable to calm himself after the tragedy, Yitzchak decided to take it upon himself to support Yisrael Jackman's widow and child. Yossi was enrolled in one of the best schools of the community while his mother had a job working for the Levinson Knitting Co.

It's a pity that people realize their mistakes too late. *Loshon hora* is so common among people that they too often forget its repercussions. Adults as well as children must remember at all times that speaking or accepting *loshon hora* is as evil as *Chazal* tell us. We should pay closer attention to the words of Dovid Hamelech in *Tehillim* (34).

"Who is the man that desires life
And loves a long life of goodness,
Guard your tongue from evil,
And your lips from speaking falsehood.
Depart from evil and do good,
Seek peace and pursue it."

תולדות

TOLDOS

❧❧❧❧

Rumors and Reality

In this week's *Parshah*, we find an amazing story of how Yitzchak was deceived by Esav, while Rivkah was not. This in itself is a great lesson: even a great person can be deceived and overestimate someone unworthy or underestimate someone worthy.

One of the most difficult laws in the Torah is not to believe *loshon hora*. Once we hear a story about someone, our natural tendency is to accept it as fact, since there is no one present at the time we hear the story to tell us it is untrue. The Torah, however, tells us not to believe it, so we tell ourselves we do not. But it is very difficult to be sincere in our disbelief of the *loshon hora*.

This issue is particularly difficult for young adults who have not as yet encountered many of life's experiences. Through experience, we learn that it is easy to be deceived. Sometimes, rumors are purposely fabricated, but more often, they come from misunderstanding. Rumors can cause much harm even when no harm is intended. Many families have suffered tremendous hardship because of false rumors, as the following story will indicate:

The great Rav Nachumke of Horodna was a giant in both Torah and *Tzedakah*. The Chafetz Chaim so admired him that he traveled far to learn from him. He kept a picture of Rav Nachumke, and when he wanted to describe a true *tzaddik*, he would point to the picture and say, "You can't imagine what a *tzaddik* he was."[32]

When Rav Nachumke was a young boy, false rumors about him caused his *Rebbe* to discontinue learning with him. Rav Nachumke was actually forced to stop learning for many years, since he could not afford another *Rebbe*.

Only after a few years was Rav Nachumke able to obtain another *Rebbe*, but soon, he was again a victim of different types of false rumors. By this time, however, he was old enough to learn on his own. He continued learning although he had to undergo the hardships of exile resulting from these rumors.[33]

In both instances, the people who spread the rumors were not gentiles. They were the kind of people we all know, the kind to whom we listen. Their words are convincing, but what they say is far from true.

Often, rumors are started through unfounded assumptions or exaggerations. Or even simple misunderstandings.

Although Moshe Rabbeinu was very wealthy, the wealth did not last in his family. His grandson Levi became poor. The people were willing to help support him, but he refused to accept handouts. He was employed as a priest for *avodah zarah*. The *Gemara*[34] explains that this choice was a result of a misunderstanding in the lessons he received from his grandfather Moshe Rabbeinu.

Moshe Rabbeinu had said that it is better to work at an alien job than to accept handouts. In Hebrew, the words for an alien job are *avodah* (job) and *zarah* (alien). The words for idol worship in Hebrew are also *avodah zarah*. Mistakenly, Levi thought idols were better than handouts.

This incredible story of Moshe's grandson is unfortunately typical of misunderstandings in our daily lives.

Written articles are more apt to be deceptive. A journalist is concerned with using flowery language and embellishing his story, which may distort facts. A classic example is the conflicting versions of the Revolutionary War in the history books of England and America, which demonstrate how "facts" are always recorded from the writer's perspective.

❧❧❧❧

Self Preservation

One may be permitted to speak *loshon hora* about oneself.[35] However, the Chafetz Chaim advised against it. This advice was given after the following experience:[36]

Returning home to Radin from one of his journeys, the Chafetz Chaim was sitting next to another Jewish passenger. The other passenger exclaimed that at last he was traveling to Radin to see the greatest *tzaddik* of the generation, the Chafetz Chaim.

This made the Chafetz Chaim very uncomfortable.

"You are making a mistake," he said. "He is far from the greatest *tzaddik* of our generation. I don't think he is even worthy of the title *tzaddik*."

This statement aggravated the passenger. He became infuriated.

"How dare you say that?" he exclaimed, and in his anger, he slapped the cheek of the Chafetz Chaim and quickly found another seat.

The train reached Radin, and a large delegation came to greet the Chafetz Chaim at the station. Suddenly, the passenger realized what he had done and almost fainted. Pale and embarrassed, he approached the Chafetz Chaim and begged his forgiveness.

"Certainly," replied the Chafetz Chaim. "You have taught me an important lesson. I never realized how harmful *loshon hora* was. This episode has taught me that one should refrain from speaking *loshon hora* even about oneself."

In our *Parshah*, we find that Yitzchak was worried. He had made a mistake by unknowingly giving the *berachos* to Yaakov. He might have taken measures to rectify this mistake had Esav not spoken about his own faults.

Esav intended to belittle Yaakov by illustrating how Yaakov had twice outsmarted him. However, Esav also harmed himself by mentioning that he had sold his birthright. This *loshon hora* was harmful to Esav, for instead of taking measures to benefit Esav, Yitzchak actually confirmed that the *berachos* should indeed go to Yaakov.[37]

ℳℳℳℳ

It Can Backfire

Not only is it prohibited to speak evil about a person, one should not even discuss another's positive qualities if doing so can bring him harm.[38]

When Yitzchak lived in the land of the Plishtim, he was wealthy. People talked about his wealth and expressed the opinion that he was richer than King Avimelech. They said that the fertilizer possessed by Yitzchak was more valuable than the gold possessed by the king.[39] Shortly thereafter, Avimelech asked Yitzchak to leave because he had become too wealthy.

ℳℳℳℳ

Ways and Means

Rivkah knew the true essence of Esav, but she never told Yitzchak her opinion. When she realized that Yitzchak wanted to give Esav a blessing which would affect the entire future of *Bnai Yisrael*, she intervened, but not by defaming Esav. She devised a more troublesome and dangerous scheme. This follows the rule that although *loshon hora* for a beneficial purpose is permitted, one should still seek an alternative method.[40]

When the furious Esav wanted to kill Yaakov, Rivkah warned Yaakov of Esav's evil intentions (as one must warn a person to protect him from danger). However, when she approached Yitzchak to send Yaakov away from the area, she did not mention Esav's evil intention.

The *Ohr Hachaim Hakadosh*[41] explains that Rivkah did not want to say *rechilus* about Esav. Since Esav did not yet openly worship idols, he was treated as a Jew in regard to the laws of *loshon hora*.

Although Rivkah had many opportunities to defame Esav, she did not. Hashem helped her accomplish her goals via other means. We are often confronted with the test of *loshon hora*. At times, we know it is best not speak our minds, although it seems to be the easiest way to accomplish our goals.

Many things we do can backfire, but if we follow the Torah, Hashem always helps. It may not be so evident at first, but it is the only way to assure true success.

ויצא

VAYETZE

❧❧❧❧

For Safety's Sake

Among the many lessons of this *Parshah* is the great reward for not speaking *loshon hora*, not only in the World to Come but also in this world.

The *Midrash* says that before Yaakov came to the house of Lavan he begged Hashem to watch him. By this he meant to guard him specifically from the sin of speaking evil, [42] which would ensure his physical safety. [43] This protection is still effective today, as can be seen from the following true story: [44]

After the long *Shabbos* morning *Shacharis* in the *Yeshiva*, Reuven did not go home right away, but first greeted his old friend Shimon. Reuven, who was still learning in the *Kollel*, sold *sefarim* on the side. Shimon had left the *Kollel* a few years before to help his father run the family business. Although Reuven was eager to eat his *Shabbos* meal, he didn't want to pass up the pleasure of chatting with Shimon, which brought him true *Shabbos* joy.

As they were speaking, Reuven told Shimon an explanation from the weekly *Parshah*, which happened to be *Vayetze*, that Yaakov prayed and pleaded with Hashem to guard him from speaking *loshon hora* so he need not fear Esav or Lavan who wanted to kill him.

"There is no better protection than not speaking *loshon hora*," Reuven concluded.

"Better than an alarm system, I'll bet," Shimon joked. "I better brush up on the laws of *loshon hora*. I'll be over at your house right after *Shabbos* to pick up a book on the subject."

"There is no great hurry," replied Reuven. "I'll bring it to you when I get a chance."

As soon as Reuven finished making *Havdalah*, he heard a knock at the door. It was Shimon.

"Didn't I tell you that you didn't need to make a special trip? I would have brought it to you," said Reuven.

"Who knows if you would have had a chance?" replied Shimon.

That week, on Wednesday afternoon, Shimon was in his father's store with his father and three customers. Suddenly, three men armed with guns entered. The bandits forced everyone to lie flat on the floor while they searched for cash.

Shimon and a customer started crawling toward the back door which had been left open. They were just outside the door when one of the robbers spotted them.

"Let's fight," the customer whispered to Shimon. "After all, there are two of us, and he is only one."

"But he has a gun," said Shimon.

"For all you know, he may shoot anyway," the customer answered.

"Keep your face down and be quiet!" ordered the robber.

Just then, a woman who lived in an apartment which overlooked the yard went to the window for air. She looked down and saw an armed robber and two victims on the ground, and began to scream, "Help! Help! Police!"

When the robber heard this, he became frightened. He ran back into the store, got his two friends and speedily escaped, leaving much cash behind.

As everyone stood up, Shimon's father said, "It is a miracle they didn't try to shoot you when you were crawling out."

"It is a miracle the lady went to the window just at the right time," added one of the customers.

"And knew just what to say," chimed in another.

"Hashem really guarded us," Shimon said. "And I know why."

He immediately went to the phone to tell Reuven what had happened and to thank him for the tip from the Chafetz Chaim for the most effective protection.

❧❧❧❧

Fruitful Results

Of Yaakov's four wives, Leah had already had many children, and even the maids had given birth. Only Rachel remained childless. Finally, Hashem remembered Rachel, and she gave birth.

Rashi[45] explains that Hashem remembered Rachel's kindness to her sister, and in that merit, she gave birth.

Lavan had tried to deceive Yaakov by giving him Leah in marriage instead of Rachel whom he desired to marry.

Yaakov had attempted to forestall any trick by developing a code with Rachel. If the bride failed to use the codes, Yaakov would know Leah had been substituted for Rachel. However, once Rachel learned that Lavan planned to substitute Leah, Rachel realized her sister would be disgraced. At great personal sacrifice, she revealed the code to her sister. Since Rachel was so concerned about her sister's dignity and honor, she was given a son.

When she gave birth, Rachel said, "Hashem has removed my disgrace." Until then, she had been embarrassed by her barrenness, but since she cared about the dignity of others, her dignity was also upheld. Even in our days, we witness similar experiences, as the following true stories illustrate:

A woman in Eretz Yisrael who was childless for nearly ten years went to a renowned *tzaddik* for a *berachah*.[46] He suggested that she become involved in getting other women to learn the laws of *loshon hora*, since this would be a merit on her behalf. Immediately, she organized a group in her town and invited lecturers to speak about *loshon hora*. She worked energetically, stopping only briefly for the birth of her first child.

When Dovid Hamelech said that whoever wants life should guard his tongue,[47] he was not necessarily referring to one's own life, but also the life of a child.

Walking on a crowded sidewalk, a mother of several children was holding her infant in her arms. Somehow, she stumbled and dropped the infant. The infant fell into a deep coma. She quickly picked him up and rushed to the hospital.

She stood in the waiting room for a few hours, praying from a small *Tehillim*. Finally, she was told that the child had suffered irreversible brain damage and would not live more than a few days. She was not willing to accept only one doctor's opinion and had other brain specialists consulted. They were all of the opinion that there was nothing to be done. She then contacted the great *tzaddikim* in Yerushalayim.

After relating all the details to one *tzaddik*, she was advised that perhaps in this desperate situation she could ask for the help of her friends. Following his instructions, she organized a group of ten women who called themselves *Machsom Lefee*, a term meaning muzzling of the mouth. Each woman agreed that for two particular hours of the day she would not get angry or speak *loshon hora*. In this way, all the waking hours of the day were covered. All was done in the merit of the sick child. To the amazement of the doctors, the child recovered completely.

Even after the recovery, the *Machsom Lefee* group continued and has brought many *berachos*.[48]

୬ଡ଼ୣ୬ଡ଼ୣ

Chillul Hashem

Toward the end of the *Parshah*, we find Yaakov leaving Lavan's house without giving notice. Lavan pursued him, and on the way, Hashem appeared to Lavan and warned him not to harm Yaakov.

Eventually, Lavan overtook Yaakov. Lavan hurled many accusations at him, openly admitting that he was powerless since Hashem had admonished him not to do anything to Yaakov.

Yaakov could have continued on his journey, ignoring Lavan. However, Yaakov answered his accusations and went to great lengths in explaining and justifying his actions. Yaakov wanted to prevent *Chillul Hashem*, for Lavan might feel that his accusations has some grains of truth and that Yaakov, Hashem's chosen one, was a liar.

In the last *Mishnah* in *Pe'ah* [49], it states that if a person pretends to be lame or blind he will eventually become truly handicapped. The *Tiferes Yisrael* explains that we are not speaking about someone who is trying to raise money because of his pretended handicap. According to the *Tiferes Yisrael*, this harsh punishment is meted out to the guilty one who diminished Hashem's glory by displaying a perfectly created person as defective. Everyone knows that there are some handicapped people in the world, but falsely portraying oneself or another as handicapped is a *Chillul Hashem* worthy of extreme punishment.

Similarly, the more people one makes aware of another person's sinning, the greater the *Chillul Hashem* one causes. Aside from speaking *loshon hora*, you are held responsible for the *Chillul Hashem* which you have caused.

※※※※

The Shield of Shame

Still another reason for not speaking *loshon hora* can be found in the explanation of the commentaries[50] on the debate between Yaakov and Lavan. Lavan asked Yaakov why he ran away without giving him a chance to kiss his grand-children and bid them farewell.

"It was foolish," he stated before receiving any reply.

How could he have been sure Yaakov had acted foolishly before hearing Yaakov's justification of his actions?

The answer is that Lavan was saying that whatever reason Yaakov might give to explain his actions would not justify the manner in which he chose to escape. Fleeing openly was to Yaakov's disadvantage.

Until now Yaakov and Lavan had given the impression that they were one close family, and naturally, Lavan would be embarrassed to harm his kin. However, now that he left in a manner which would indicate that Lavan was his foe, Yaakov had removed the embarrassment. Harming Yaakov was now within the realm of possibility.

The *Akeidas Yitzchak*[51] points out many places in *Tan-ach* where we find that once a person was suspected of doing a certain action, the suspicion gave him the excuse to do that which before had been impossible.

Falsely broadcasting that someone has harmed us may not only be *loshon hora* but it can now make it easier for the harm to come about, for now it is no longer embarrassing.

❦❦❦❦

Sensitivity to Others' Feelings

The *Ohr Hachaim Hakadosh* [52] explains that when Yaakov replied to Lavan, he called Lavan aside and spoke to him privately, so as not to embarrass Lavan. Yaakov was so careful about the feelings of others, even Lavan, who had accused him and embarrassed him publicly.

The following story illustrates how sensitive we must be to another person's feelings: [53]

It was the happiest day in the life of Rav Baruch Ber Leibowitz, the *Rosh Yeshiva* of Kaminetz. For many years, he had been looking for a *shidduch* for his oldest daughter, and at last, his prayers were answered.

A learned *bachur* in the *Yeshiva*, Yitzchak Meisel, was going to marry his daughter. Yitzchak was not only learned but was also handsome and personable. Before the engagement was made official, the *Rosh Yeshiva* bought Yitzchak a new suit, a new coat and a golden watch.

After the official *Tena'im*, the *Rosh Yeshiva* called in his future son-in-law and said that since it is not customary for the prospective *Chasan* and *Kalla* to see each other before the wedding, he should temporarily learn in the Volozhiner Yeshiva until the day of the wedding, when he would return to Kaminetz.

Shortly after Yitzchak arrived in Volozhin, he was approached by the city *shadchan*. Yitzchak had made a very favorable impression on the wealthy Mr. Gevirtz, who wanted him to marry his daughter. Yitzchak told the matchmaker that it was too late, since he was already engaged to the daughter of Rav Baruch Ber.

"Don't you want to continue learning Torah for the rest of your life?" the matchmaker argued. "You realize that the poor *Rosh Yeshiva* won't be able to support you for long, whereas the wealthy Mr. Gevirtz insists he is willing and able to support you for the rest of your life."

After many attempts, the matchmaker was finally successful in convincing Yitzchak that he had made a mistake in taking the daughter of Rav Baruch Ber. He would do better to nullify the agreement and try for Mr. Gevirtz's daughter.

To be sure Mr. Gevirtz would accept him, the matchmaker advised Yitzchak to obtain some letter from his former city to acknowledge his high status in learning.

Yitzchak sent back the new suit, coat and watch to Rav Baruch Ber, with a letter explaining that the marriage to his daughter was not obligatory and that he had changed his mind. He continued by making the outrageous request that the *Rosh Yeshiva* send him a letter he could show to his next prospect, who was not familiar with his learning status.

When Rav Baruch Ber received the letter, he was heartbroken. His daughter and wife burst into tears. To make matters worse, making the engagement and then breaking it would make it even more difficult to find someone else in the future. Rav Baruch Ber felt, in addition to his own personal grief, the family's deep anguish as well.

The next day, Rav Baruch Ber called one of his *bachurim*, Koppel Kelemer, and asked him to bring in the *Mashgiach* and two of the best *bachurim* in the *Yeshiva* (one was Rav Shlomo Heiman, the future *Rosh Yeshiva* of Torah Vodaath).

When they came into the room, Rav Baruch Ber asked them, "Do you remember Yitzchak Meisel?"

"Of course," they replied.

"Please listen to the description I have written of his learning status," said Rav Baruch Ber.

He then read his letter which gave a very complimentary assessment of Yitzchak. He asked those present to tell him if he had left out anything whatsoever, or if the description was an understatement and it would be appropriate to add more.

His action seemed strange. The *Rosh Yeshiva* was not accustomed to doing this in other instances. He explained that he feared that for personal reasons, he might leave out compliments which Yitzchak deserved to receive. A deficient description is also *loshon hora*.

Young Koppel, who lived in Rav Baruch Ber's house and was aware of what was going on, stood at the side, amazed and nearly crying. Not only had the great Rav consented to grant a letter to a person who had caused him such sorrow, he had done it with such care and caution, so as not to violate the laws of *loshon hora*. It was a demonstration of self control *par excellence.*

וישלח

VAYISHLACH

❧❧❧❧❧

Profitable Preparations

After Yaakov sent a large gift to his brother Esav and prepared the camp for war, he prayed to Hashem.

"Save me from the hands of my brother, from the hands of Esav," he asked Hashem.

The *Zohar*[54] asks that since Yaakov only had one brother, why did he have to mention him by name?

The answer is that although prayers can be understood when not explicit, one should nevertheless be as specific as possible when praying. One should prepare and choose his expressions carefully before prayer.

Preparation is an important factor. The *Midrash* says[55] that whenever Rav Yanai needed to deal with the Roman government, he would first read the *Parshah* of *Vayishlach* in order to prepare himself to follow Yaakov's pattern of dealing with the wicked descendants of Esav (Rome). On one occasion he did not prepare, and the mission was not successful.

The laws dealing with *loshon hora* are numerous. At

times, we may be obligated to forestall a friend's loss by making him aware of certain dangers.[56] However, before speaking to him, it pays to prepare not only by reviewing the laws, but also by choosing which terms to use.

It is beneficial to first write down what one plans to say and then check for possible exaggerations or unfounded assumptions. If this is not possible, one must simply decide carefully what to say. The advantage of careful preparation is illustrated in the following story:[57]

M any years ago there lived two great Torah scholars. One was Rav Yaakov, author of *Nesivos Hamishpat*, and the other was an author of numerous *sefarim*. The *Nesivos Hamishpat* became an instant best seller, a true Torah classic. The other author's books were also accepted, but their success did not compare to the *Nesivos*.

Once, when both authors met, the other author asked Rav Yaakov why his *sefer* met with so much popularity, whereas his own did not.

"I don't know," Rabbi Yaakov replied. "But perhaps you can tell me what your daily learning schedule is?"

"I arise early when my head is clear and write my thoughts even before I go to *shul*," Rabbi Aryeh Leib replied. "After returning from *shul* and eating, I devote a few hours to learning, and the next few hours I continue to write. I also divide my afternoon between learning and writing. At night, I finish writing whatever I may not have had the opportunity to write during the day."

"That explains it," said Rav Yaakov. "My schedule is almost identical, but there is one small difference. In the early morning, I write just as you do. However, after I return from *shul* and learn, I examine what I have written and cross out whatever I have to. In the afternoon I reexamine and cross out more. At night I cross out whatever I am still not sure about."

ᴊᴊᴊᴊ

Reimbursement of Time

Before sending a letter, it is advisable to check if it has any *loshon hora*. The *Yetzer Hora* may say that it is troublesome and time consuming. However, the truth is that no time will actually be lost by doing so, as the following story demonstrates:[58]

In the *Yeshiva* of Radin, the Chafetz Chaim wanted to start a free loan organization for the *bachurim* to be efficiently run by a reliable *bachur*. When he approached the student he considered most qualified and offered him this *mitzvah*, the student refused.

Noticing the Chafetz Chaim's puzzled expression, the student explained, "I know that such a job will cause much distraction from my studies. I have much to accomplish and insufficient time to work over the books and make the loans. I want to be able to accomplish my goals."

"If this is all," the Chafetz Chaim reassured him, "you'll have plenty of time. You remember, I am sure, that the sons of Eli Hakohen sinned, and Hashem told Shmuel Hanavi that their punishment would be death in battle and that all their descendants would not live beyond the age of eighteen.[59] The only exceptions would be those who engaged in the study of Torah. The *Gemara*[60] relates that both Abaye and Rava were descendants of Eli. Abaye, who engaged only in the study of Torah, lived to the age of forty. However, Rava, who engaged in the study of Torah and also in acts of kindness, lived sixty years. Therefore, if you take care of the free loan, you will be blessed with many more years in which to accomplish more in learning."

Long before the Chafetz Chaim lived, Dovid Hamelech promised life to all those who guard themselves from *loshon hora.*[61] The time it takes to be sure you don't speak *loshon hora* will certainly be repaid.

※※※※

Keeping One's Distance

When Esav offered to escort Yaakov, Yaakov refused. He knew that associating with Esav would not lead to any good. Indeed, when Yaakov met and overcame the angel representing Esav, he still suffered. In addition to not associating with evil persons, it is also advisable to keep our distant from those who are ignorant of the laws of *loshon hora*, as can be seen from the following story:[62]

The Chasam Sofer was the *Rosh Yeshiva* of Pressburg and also served as *Rav* of the town. Despite being busy day and night, he helped people all over the world, responding to difficult *Halachic* questions and helping those in financial need. At the same time, he fought a fierce battle against the Reform movement.

Finally, the strain began to show, and his doctors told him to take a vacation. He followed their advice and went to a vacation resort called Angeren, where he stayed in a bungalow. A wealthy man who was staying in a nearby bungalow invited the Chasam Sofer to come and stay with him, since he wanted the honor of this famous *Gaon* staying in his house. He constantly pleaded and begged the Chasam Sofer and offered him anything he requested.

Finally, the Chasam Sofer consented to his request but on the condition that he have a room to stay in by himself. The Chasam Sofer would tend to everything himself, and for all practical purposes he would be living alone. The wealthy man happily agreed and quickly provided him with a comfortable room.

When *Shabbos* arrived, the Chasam Sofer greeted his host and his family with a hearty "Good *Shabbos*" and went directly to his room.

The wealthy man decided to observe the Chasam Sofer. He went to the room and crouched in front of the door. He had a clear view through the large, old-fashioned keyhole. He then saw a strange sight. The Chasam Sofer made *Kiddush* and instantly made the *berachah Hamotzi* on the *Challah* without bothering to wash. He was amazed. "After all," thought the wealthy man. "I myself had brought a wash basin to the room. The Chasam Sofer could have washed if he would have cared to trouble himself to get up. Now I see that the Chasam Sofer is not what they make him to be. He is lax in keeping the *mitzvos* when no one is around. Maybe that is why he likes to stay alone."

He left the door and related his discovery to his family. They shared this gossip with their friends.

The man no longer wanted to have the Chasam Sofer as his guest, and after Shabbos, he withdrew his invitation.

The Chasam Sofer realized what had happened.

"It is my fault," he said. "Our *Chachamim* warn us to be careful about associating with the unlearned. This is why I refused to stay here at first. However, seeing that it meant so much to you, I wanted to make you feel good. I hoped that if I would stay in my own room, I wouldn't need to worry. However, I was mistaken."

The Chasam Sofer then explained.

"I keep all the customs of Frankfurt," he said. "That is why I always wash before *Kiddush*. When you watched me through the keyhole, I had already washed, and therefore, you thought you saw me eat bread without washing. You did not know that there are two opinions in the *Shulchan Aruch* [63] as to how *Kiddush* should be made. Yet, you immediately jumped to conclusions and spread *loshon hora*. I have learned my lesson and in the future will be more careful about associating with the unlearned."

༺༺༺

The Friendly Foe

After Esav accepted Yaakov's gifts, he offered to escort Yaakov. Yaakov, however, refused, knowing that at times the enemy will plant a trap with false friendship and that one must always be on the alert.

We too must always be on the alert in our battle with the *Yetzer Hora*. Even if we are successful, we must always be cautious.

The Chafetz Chaim explains the meaning of our asking Hashem every evening to "remove the Satan from in front of us and from behind us." The Satan in front of us refers to the Satan that is an obvious enemy. The one behind us refers to the one who may pat us on the back and urge us to do *mitzvos*. However, his only intent is to trap us when we are unaware and unsuspecting.

We can only combat him if we always remain on guard, as the following story shows:

The Chozeh of Lublin lived in a different city from his student the Yid Hakadosh. Rumors started spreading that the Yid was going against his *Rebbe* and starting his own sect of *Chassidus*. At that time, there lived a *chassid* named Rav Kusiel, who had a reputation for not speaking *loshon hora* for over forty years. He also testified against the Yid.

When the Yid got wind of this he went to the Chozeh. After the Yid explained the source of the misunderstanding, the Chozeh was convinced the accusations were false.

At that time the Chozeh said that the Satan had protected Rav Kusiel from speaking *loshon hora* for the past forty years, so that when the time came to speak against the Yid, everyone would believe him.

וישב

VAYAISHEV

❧❧❧❧

Measure for Measure

In this *Parshah*, we find the sad story of how Yosef and his brothers suffered as a result of *loshon hora*. When Yosef's brothers seemed to act improperly, he did not rebuke them personally. Instead, he brought evil reports to his father. The suffering he went through to atone for this sin corresponded to the sin measure for measure.[65] Just as he spread false rumors about his brothers, false rumors were spread about him by the wife of Potifera when he was in Egypt. This scandal was the talk of the land for a long time, until Pharaoh's head butler and baker were placed in the same jail as Yosef. At last the topic of gossip changed.[66]

Yosef's brothers also made the mistake of falsely accusing Yosef. This resulted in their attempt to kill him. As a result, they suffered great anguish until Yosef finally revealed himself to them.

Indeed, because of the episode of Yosef and his brothers, we still suffer today. Every *Yom Kippur* and *Tisha b'Av* we recite the *Payit*[67] which tells us that the ten great sages were tortured to death during the time of the second *Bais Hamikdash* to atone for the sin of Yosef's brothers.

Rav Elchanan Wasserman[68] writes that the Jewish nation suffered from blood libels throughout the generations because of the staining of Yosef's cloak with blood before sending it to Yaakov. A short analysis of the blood libel can show how it is related to the sin of *loshon hora*.

For centuries, the gentiles repeatedly fabricated a ridiculous story saying that Jews murder gentiles in order to obtain blood for their *matzos*. To avenge this supposed practice, the gentiles killed many hundreds of Jews. Although the gentiles were proven wrong time and again, the blood libels continued to cause mass murders for many centuries.

It is well known that one of the reasons the Jewish people are in exile is because of the sin of *loshon hora*. Since we were guilty of accepting accusations about others, therefore, we were punished with the public believing false accusations concerning us.

It is difficult not to believe *loshon hora*. Many times we tell ourselves that we do not believe it, but after a few days, we somehow feel it is true. By the same token, the blood libels, refuted many times still kept creeping up with claims to truth and thus became believable. We should realize that believing *loshon hora* a long time after our decision not to believe it is just as forbidden and can be just as devastating as believing it immediately.

Synchronizing with Satan

We find in this *Parshah* that Yaakov sent Yosef to
·Shechem to report on the welfare of his brothers. When he
arrived in Shechem, his brothers had already left. Yosef
could have returned home then, and he would have been
spared all his misfortune. However, it "happened" that he
met a man who "happened" to know just where his brothers
were. *Rashi*[69] states that the "man" was actually the good
angel Gavriel. Sometimes it seems as if Satan is also successful in manipulating things to his advantage. The following
tale is a good example:[70]

One of the great European *Roshei Yeshiva* came to
America and opened a *Yeshiva* which met with
great success. In fact, it is now one of the largest *Yeshivos* in
the world. He was a scholar of the highest caliber who
memorized volumes upon volumes of *sefarim*. He once
mentioned the following experience.

This *Rosh Yeshiva* made it a practice always to take along
a *sefer* and look into it as he traveled on the subway, not to
give the impression that he was just sitting idly. One day, he
had to leave suddenly and did not pick up a *sefer* as he
rushed out. As he sat on the subway train reviewing by
memory the lecture he was going to give that day, he
overheard two men sitting on the seat next to him
conversing.

"Those old European Rabbis!" they said. "When I was a
young child in Europe, I saw them spend all their time
learning. Now they come to America and idle away time."

The point, he stressed, was that all the other times he took the *sefer* with him no one may have noticed, but the time he forgot to take his *sefer*, it made a difference. Unfortunately, Satan had succeeded.

In the following parable, remarks made during a "chance" meeting, doubtlessly arranged by Satan, had drastic effects on a family's livelihood:[71]

R abbi Gunthoff was a very popular *Rebbe* who taught the fifth grade in a local day school. He and his large family were very helpful in building a fine Torah community. Their example of true kindness and friendship was greatly appreciated by all who knew them.

Unfortunately, Rabbi Gunthoff became ill. Although he recovered, his vocal cords were affected, and the doctors told him he could no longer teach, for constantly speaking in a classroom would be very dangerous for him. This was indeed sad news for Rabbi Gunthoff, for he enjoyed teaching more than anything else. However, he understood that all that transpires is for the best.

The only trade he knew was the one he had learned from his father and grandfather who had been bakers. He had spent much time as a boy in his father's bakery, and he had become an excellent baker. He would have preferred using his teaching talents, but there was no choice.

Opening a bakery was not simple, for he did not have much money. He borrowed from everyone he could till he could at last buy a store, ovens, pans, and so forth. He needed more money, but he had already borrowed all he could. He could not afford to buy superior flour. He could only purchase inferior flour and other ingredients at discount prices.

The first day, he had many customers who came to try the new shop. However, since he was forced to use inferior ingredients, he could only produce inferior pastry. He realized he could not continue in this manner. He would have to take out a loan and invest it in good quality ingredients, but from whom?

Mr. Good, a wealthy merchant, walked into the store. Rabbi Gunthoff wondered, "Mr. Good moved out of town years ago. Why did he come to my store today? Perhaps . . . What can I lose?"

He greeted Mr. Good, asking him what brought him to these parts.

"I was just passing by," said Mr. Good. "I got hungry and saw a kosher bakery shop."

"Maybe you came by to do a *mitzvah*," Rabbi Gunthoff said. He explained to Mr. Good how he had been sick and could not teach and was forced to open up this shop. He also told Mr. Good that he was not finished setting up yet, and perhaps he could grant him a loan that he needed. "You can rest assured I will repay you as soon as I get established."

"Let me first pay you for these buns," said Mr. Good. "But to make the loan, I'll have to get the checkbook from my car."

On his way to the car, he met an old friend.

"*Shalom Aleichem*, what brings you here?" asked the friend.

"I was passing through on a business trip, and I saw the kosher bakery," said Mr. Good. "But I was surprised to see Rabbi Gunthoff as the proprietor."

"It's a sad story," the friend said. "But, you know, he was a much better teacher than baker. His products are not very tasty. I am not the only one who feels this way. I think he would have more success at earning a livelihood by trying something else.I don't think this shop will last long."

When Mr. Good heard this, he had second thoughts about the loan. He looked at his watch and said, "Excuse me. I must be on my way." He got into his car and drove off quickly.

It took Rabbi Gunthoff a month to get the loan he needed, but it was too late. His store already had a reputation for inferior quality goods. After struggling for a while, he had to sell the store and work in a factory for a low wage, part of which was used to repay outstanding debts. One thoughtless comment from Mr. Good's friend at the most inappropriate time brought great hardship to Rabbi Gunthoff's family for many years.

܍܍܍܍

Self-Unveiling

The wife of Potifera accused Yosef of committing the sin of adultery. The truth was just the opposite. She herself was guilty of the sin of which she accused Yosef. This is often typical of those who speak *loshon hora*. The accuser is guilty of the fault with which he tries to brand others.

The *Gemara*[72] states a rule that one who finds fault with other people's lineage has improper lineage himself.

Rav Yehudah once sent a messenger to purchase meat from the butcher shop in the city of Pumbedisa. While he was being served, another customer who had traveled from a different city demanded to be served first. The butcher told him to be patient and wait his turn until the messenger of Rav Yehudah the son of Yechezkel was first served.

"Who is the son of Tiskoll that he should come before me?" exclaimed the visitor deliberately distorting the name.

The messenger returned to Rav Yehudah and complained about the visitor's disgraceful behavior and suggested he be reprimanded and punished.

Rabbi Yehudah investigated and uncovered the fact that this man had a habit of calling other persons gentile slaves. Rabbi Yehudah had the visitor excommunicated as a result of his disgraceful behavior in the butcher shop and proclaimed that he was a gentile slave. Consequently, no one should marry into his family.

The infuriated visitor returned to Neharda'a and had the *Rav* summon Rav Yehudah to his court on charges of being unjustly punished. When Rav Yehudah arrived, he observed many unintentional mistakes that the *Rav* of Neharda'a was making and brought them to his attention. The *Rav* of Neharda'a was thankful for the criticism and realized his inferiority to Rav Yehudah's scholarly status.

He apologized and confessed that since Rav Yehudah was a far greater scholar, he had acted improperly by summoning him. However, he wished to understand how he could brand someone a slave, and prohibit marriage into his family, just because he was not careful with his tongue?

Rav Yehudah answered that there is a rule that when one accuses others of improper lineage, this is a proof that his lineage is in the same improper status he attributes to others.

"Since I have investigated and found that he accuses others of being gentile slaves, I know that he is one," said Rav Yehudah.

After further investigation, it was discovered that the man was, indeed, a descendant of gentile slaves. On that day, all those who had previously married into his family were forced to separate from their spouses.

We all know the famous adage that "misery loves company." For this reason, no handicapped person was permitted in the army of Yisrael. A handicapped person will not be as troubled if others suffer the same fate and he may not try to defend them sufficiently.

According to the Torah, every fifty years, when the *Yovel* arrives, the *shofar* is sounded, signaling freedom to all Jewish slaves.[73] The *Chinuch*[74] explains that this is done because the owners feel sad about the detrimental effect their slaves' freedom may have on their livelihoods. Hearing the *shofar* blast reminds the owners that everyone else is making the same sacrifice, and they are comforted.

Even if you feel soothed when you accuse others by proclaiming their faults, it does not pay to speak *loshon hora*, for you may be incriminating yourself. You may cause others to have bad opinions about you and they will suspect you are only trying to cover your own faults.

❧❧❧❧

Occupational Threat and Therapy

There are various commentaries regarding the faults Yosef related to his father in his reports. The *Sforno* explains[75] that Yosef complained the brothers tended the sheep improperly, thereby compromising their main source of income, which was herding sheep. Stating that someone does an inefficient job without a good reason is *loshon hora*[76], and such statements can often cause irreparable damage, as the following tale illustrates:

A lady was unhappy about the cool treatment she received from the local butcher. She was so disturbed that she started spreading rumors about the *kashrus* of the meat.[77]

One of her friends, who was aware of what was behind her words, rebuked her strongly. When she returned home, she found a fire had broken out while she was away. No one was hurt, but she suffered great financial loss. She recognized the Divine Hand of Hashem and related her financial loss to the financial loss she was causing others.

She approached the *Rav* of the town to seek advice and to prevent further suffering. The *Rav* noted that she was too weak to fast long fasts so he suggested a different course of action. She should take a slaughtered chicken and pluck all the feathers. The next day, she should come to the *Rav*. At every step, she should place a feather, until they were all gone.

The woman followed the *Rav's* directions. When she arrived at the *Rav's* house, he told her to go back and collect each feather she had dropped.

In a short while, she returned to the *Rav* in tears, unable to fulfill his prescribed method of repentance, since almost all the feathers were blown away.

"Likewise, even if you attempt to go back to your friends and confess that you wrongly defamed the butcher, it won't correct the problem," said the *Rav*. "False rumors spread faster than blowing feathers and are just as irretrievable."

מקץ

MIKAYTZ

❧❧❧❧❧

Is It Really Worth It?

After his release from prison, the butler finally remembered Yosef and told Pharaoh about Yosef's ability to interpret dreams. At the same time he insulted Yosef in every manner possible. *Rashi* explains that he degraded him by saying he was a foolish slave who could not speak the Egyptian language.

Rashi[78] introduces the words of the butler with the following statement: "Cursed are the wicked, for even the good they perform is blemished."

Many times, we do someone a favor in a mean manner. We justify it to ourselves by thinking that our favor far outweighs any harm we may do. This is the way of the wicked.

Sometimes, this extends to the family. A parent can feel he brings so much welfare to his children that he need not be careful about the way he speaks about them. A husband may feel he does so much for his wife that he can speak about her as he pleases. And vice versa. The Torah, however, requires a person to be more careful about the feelings of his family than about those of others.[79]

❧❧❧❧

The High Cost of Experience

When Yosef's brothers came to Egypt to buy food, he could have told them immediately that he was Yosef and invited them to come to Egypt for the duration of the famine. Why was it necessary for Yosef to hide his identity and allow his brothers to go through so much hardship before he finally revealed himself?

Yosef wanted to help his brothers repent. This they could not do without realizing the magnitude of anguish their sin had caused.

The Chafetz Chaim explains[80] at length how the tribes' suffering corresponded to their sins. For instance, *Rashi*[81] states that Levi was first to open the food sacks Yosef sold them on the return journey from Egypt. He found the money that was supposed to have been used as payment for the food. When he told his brothers, they were all terrified, and exclaimed, "What has Hashem done to us?"

Since Levi was first to incite the brothers against Yosef, calling him a dreamer and suggesting he be killed, he was also the first to suffer the shock of finding the unwanted money in his sack. Then, he had something else to talk to his brothers about.

Similarly, every detail of the incidents which occurred,

from the first time the brothers came to Egypt until Yosef revealed his identity to them, corresponded to their sins and helped them repent. The brothers were certainly aware they had been wrong, but to do proper *teshuvah*, they needed to feel and sense it.

There is an awesome lesson for us to learn from the brothers' experiences. We all know that *loshon hora* is the cause of much hardship. If we would really *feel* it, we would certainly not speak it. However, if we, Heaven forbid, do speak it, then perhaps for our own good, we may have to endure hardships to enable us to truly repent. It would be wise to avoid learning this lesson the hard way. The easy way is "Don't speak *loshon hora!*"

ויגש

VAYIGASH

❦❦❦❦

Triumphant Tongue

When Yehudah approaches Yosef and recounts recent incidents, the Torah repeats each word of his long speech. It was this heartwarming speech which encouraged Yosef to reveal himself. As we can see, words are quite powerful. While evil speech was the cause of the problems of the brothers, good speech was the remedy. A famous story is told herewith:[82]

M any years ago, there lived a great and powerful king in a distant country. The king was kind to his subjects, and they all loved him.

One day, the king became gravely ill. All the best doctors in the kingdom were called, and one after another, they left the king's chamber in despair. None of them knew a cure for the king's illness. Finally, the last of the doctors had left.

The king's chief physician, who had stayed at his bedside throughout the illness, said to him, "Actually, there is one cure for His Majesty's illness. I heard of it many years ago."

"What?" said the king. "Why didn't you say anything before this? Don't you see I'm dying?"

"I didn't tell you sooner," said the physician sadly, "because the cure must be made from the milk of a lioness. How in the world can one get milk from a lioness? What lioness would let someone milk her?"

A moan of despair spread throughout the king's chamber. Kuntar, one of the king's most faithful servants had been wondering how he could help his unfortunate master. Suddenly, he had an idea.

"If I will be given ten sheep and enough food and drink for a two-week journey," he said, "I'll bring back the milk of a lioness!"

The king immediately dispatched the other servants to fulfill Kuntar's request, and they did so speedily with the greatest of joy.

Quickly, ten sheep and a sack filled with food were assembled for Kuntar at the palace gate. With the good wishes and blessings of the king and all his subjects, Kuntar started on his way. He walked for a few hours and finally reached the outskirts of the kingdom. He continued walking, and by nightfall, he came to the edge of a dark and frightening forest filled with the sounds of wild animals and birds. There, at the edge of the forest, Kuntar lit a fire and spent the night.

As soon as the sun came up, Kuntar continued on his way. As he was walking with his sheep through the forest, Kuntar heard the roaring of lions. He stopped, tied nine of the sheep to a tree, took the tenth sheep and started walking towards the roaring lions. In a few minutes, a pride of roaring lions came into view.

Filled with fear, Kuntar picked up the sheep in his arms and walked over ever so softly towards the lions' den. Suddenly, one of the lions caught sight of Kuntar. He roared and advanced towards the frightened but faithful servant of the king. Immediately, Kuntar threw the sheep to the lion. Then, he turned and ran for his life.

Finally, Kuntar stopped running. He turned around and saw that the sheep was gone. He heard the lions roaring, obviously with pleasure, for they had eaten a delicious meal.

Each of the next few days, Kuntar again approached the lions' den, and each day, he came a bit closer to the lions. By the fourth day, the lions didn't even roar. They just waited for Kuntar to deliver their delicious meal.

By the sixth day, Kuntar came close enough to the lions to touch them. They knew that Kuntar would not hurt them, and besides, he brought them a daily delicacy.

By the eighth day, Kuntar stayed to play with the lions after their meal. And the ninth day, he played with them, too.

Finally, on the tenth day, after they had eaten the last of the sheep, Kuntar quietly and gently approached a mother lioness. Slowly, he sat down beside her and milked her very cautiously so as not to spill a drop.

Kuntar carefully closed the jug of the lion's milk. Happy and relieved, he began his journey home.

He walked out of the forest, through the clearing, and continued until he saw the houses of the kingdom. Although he was thoroughly exhausted, he was so happy and proud that he had obtained the milk that would cure the king that he kept on walking. How happy the king would be, he thought, and he, the king's most faithful servant, would be greatly honored and richly rewarded.

Presently, Kuntar felt so weak that he needed to rest. After carefully placing the jug of milk on the ground, Kuntar lay down and fell into a deep, deep sleep. And in his sleep, he had a dream.

Kuntar began to dream that the different parts of his body were fighting with each other.

His feet, looking very haughty and proud, said, "Among all the limbs, there are none as courageous as we are. If we hadn't walked through the forest to the lion's den, there wouldn't be any milk in that jug. And the king would have died!"

"Huh!" answered the hands. "What good would all your walking have done if we hadn't milked the lion? Surely, we're more important than you."

"Foolish hands!" the head cried out in protest. "Foolish feet! It was I who thought of this whole idea. If not for my plan you would have been of no use whatsoever. I'm far more important than all of you."

Then the quiet voice of the tongue was heard.

"Aren't you forgetting something?" said the tongue. "If I had not spoken, the king would never even have heard of the plan, and the plan would never have been carried out. So—"

Before the tongue could finish, all the other limbs started shouting at him, "Aren't you ashamed to be so conceited and proud?"

In less than a moment's time, the tongue had an answer for the jealous limbs.

"If that's what you think," said the tongue, "then today, when we stand before the king, I'll show you that I, the weak

little tongue, without even a single bone, am more important than all of you together!"

Suddenly, Kuntar awoke and realized he had fallen asleep.
It was starting to get dark, so Kuntar picked up the jug of
milk and rushed towards the king's palace.

Quickly, he arrived at the palace gate, and moments later,
he was ushered into the chamber of the king. Standing
beside his bed with the jug of lion's milk in his hands, Kuntar
blurted out with pride and excitement, "Your majesty, I
have brought you the milk of a dog!"

Before Kuntar had a chance to correct what he had said,
the poor, sick king shouted at Kuntar in disappointment and
rage.

"How dare you ridicule the king!?" cried the king. "You
said you'd bring me the milk of a lion. For what did I give you
ten sheep? And for what have I waited these many days?
Certainly not for the milk of a dog!"

In a furious rage, the king ordered his soldiers to put
Kuntar into prison for the night and to hang him in the
morning.

Throughout this ordeal, Kuntar's tongue refused to speak
up. The king's soldiers tied Kuntar's hands and feet and
threw him into prison, as the king had commanded. Once
there, he was overcome with sorrow, fright and confusion.
Still exhausted, Kuntar once again fell into a deep, deep
sleep. Once again, he had a dream.

This time, he dreamed that all the parts of his body were
feeling terribly sad and broken.

"Why have you done this to us?" they cried out to the
tongue. "Why have you brought us death with your words?
Why? Why?"

93

"So now, you see who your leader is," the tongue answered in triumph. "Admit it!"

"Yes, we admit it," all the parts of the body said. "We do. We know now that you're our leader."

"And now," said the tongue, "you will see that I can not only bring you death but also life."

Early the next morning, Kuntar was awakened by the clanging of the prison door. He opened his eyes and saw the soldiers who had come to hang him.

Immediately, Kuntar begged them to let him see the king before he died. He pleaded and begged until finally they agreed.

Kuntar was brought into the king's chamber. He ran to the king's bedside and pleaded, "Oh, your majesty, don't have me killed. There's been a mistake! I did bring you the cure you need! I know I said it was the milk of a dog, but it was a mistake. I was tired and confused from the journey. I had meant that the lion had been as gentle as a dog. I trained it to be as gentle as a dog in order to obtain its milk for you, your majesty. But truly, I promise you, it's the milk of a lion. I risked my life to bring it to you. You must believe me!"

Kuntar's words were so sincere that the king ordered his servants to examine the milk to determine whether it was the milk of a lion or a dog. In a short while, the servant returned to the king's chamber and informed him the milk was indeed the milk of a lion. The king was very happy. He drank the milk, every last drop, and soon became well again.

The king, grateful for having his health restored, rewarded his faithful servant Kuntar with great honor and wealth. Kuntar and his family lived the rest of their lives in happiness and tranquility.

And who did Kuntar have to thank besides the king? His tongue. His tongue had almost killed him by speaking false words, but when his tongue spoke the truth, it saved his life and the life of the king.

꙳꙳꙳꙳

The Worst Kind

At the time Yosef revealed himself to his brothers, he did not want to disgrace them in front of the Egyptians, for the worst form of *loshon hora* is embarrassing a person.[83] Although Yosef was endangering himself by having his Egyptian guards and the rest of the court leave when he was about to reveal his identity, he was willing to risk his life rather then embarrass his brothers. This was indeed a risk, since just two of his brothers had been able to kill the population of the city of Shechem, all ten brothers would have easily been able to kill him, had they so desired.

꙳꙳꙳꙳

Leprosy or Poverty

After Yosef had revealed himself, he told his brothers that he would feed them and their families.

Rashi[84] explains that when the brothers first went to

95

Egypt, they actually had ample food but were unwilling to appear in better straits than their starving neighbors. Eventually, their supply also ceased, and they were forced to return a second time to Egypt. This time, it was a matter of life and death. Only after doing *teshuvah* for the entire affair with Yosef did they again have a means of sustaining themselves.

The Chafetz Chaim writes[85] that the punishment for speaking *loshon hora* (when leprosy laws do not apply) is poverty. We see how the brothers were subjected to poverty until they repented for their sin, which began when they spoke *loshon hora* to one another against Yosef.

The following story relays the message to us that *loshon hora* can cause poverty in modern times also:[86]

The Chasam Sofer in his younger years was the student of Rav Nassan Adler, a very righteous and great scholar, who never forgot anything he learned.

Some of Rav Adler's actions, however, were misunderstood by the ignorant. For instance, being a *kohain*, he would *duchen* (pronounce the blessing of the *kohanim*) every day. This practice is usually done only on *YomTov*, outside of Eretz Yisrael.

Some of the ignorant townspeople considered him peculiar and tried to drive him from the town by building up a strong opposition to him. Rav Nassan Adler was a man who could not tolerate any strife, especially if he was the cause of it. Although he was innocent, he left the city of Boskowitz and returned to his home town where everyone knew and respected him. Wherever he went, his loyal student, the Chasam Sofer, followed.

Years passed, and Rav Adler passed away. The Chasam Sofer became a renowned *Rav*. The needy would come to his house with their problems and to seek financial aid. Despite a taxing schedule, the Chasam Sofer helped his needy visitors speedily and efficiently.

Once, he spent an unusually long time with a needy man. The man himself marvelled at the special treatment. He apologized and told the Chasam Sofer that he could not help but wonder why the Chasam Sofer spent so much more time with him than with other people.

The Chasam Sofer first gave him a donation and a letter so that he could be more successful in his collections. Then he replied.

"I remember when you lived in the city of Boskowitz during the time my great teacher Rav Nassan Adler lived there," said the Chasam Sofer. "You are well aware that you and others spoke against him and finally caused him to leave that town. I once asked how a person like him, who devoted his life to the service of Hashem, should suffer so and those who disgraced him should not be punished for their terrible deeds.

"He answered that the day will come when all of them would be knocking at my door, for they would become the victims of poverty. Rav Nassan Adler was well versed in the *Zohar* and knew the punishment it designates to those who speak *loshon hora*.

"Many years passed, and just what my teacher predicted happened. I kept track of the people who persecuted him, and they all became poor. That is, everyone except you. I was often bothered how my teacher could foresee accurately all that would happen. However, today, when you came, I marveled at how the great Rabbi Adler perceived even the smallest details."

❊❊❊❊

Good News

After twenty years of mourning, Yaakov was rewarded to hear exciting news, tidings that brought more joy than anything else. The Torah states that when he heard it, he was not able to believe it. It was too good to be true.

Since he did not believe the evil reports Yosef spoke concerning his brothers,[87] he was rewarded to hear the unbelievable good news—that Yosef was still alive.

❊❊❊❊

True Repentance

Upon Yaakov's arrival in Egypt, Yosef was overcome with joy. He personally hitched his horses to his chariot and went to greet his father. However, Yosef settled his father in the land of Goshen. He sent his son Ephraim there to learn from Yaakov, but he himself gave up the opportunity of learning from his father for something more important. The *Meforshim*[88] explain that Yosef did not want to give Yaakov the opportunity to ask him what had happened to him when he left. This would bring Yosef to the temptation of speaking ill about his brothers. This was Yosef's ultimate repentance for his youthful sin of bringing evil tidings—*loshon hora*.

וַיְחִי

VAYECHI

❧❧❧❧

Valuable Words

This *Parshah* tells of the *berachos* Yaakov gave his children before his death. His *berachos* were everlasting since Yaakov was very careful with his tongue. From this *parshah* we learn the power of a blessing given by one who guards his tongue. When someone is very careful with his words, Hashem empowers all his words with greater meaning and effect. Many recorded incidents demonstrate this fact.

A five year old girl was playing in the streets of Radin, not far from the home of the Chafetz Chaim.[89] A rabbi, who had just heard exciting news, was hurrying to share his good fortune with the Chafetz Chaim. He nearly stumbled over the girl.

In his excitement, he grabbed the child's hand and said, "Come, let us get a *berachah* from the Chafetz Chaim."

After sharing the good tidings with the Chafetz Chaim, he asked him to give a *berachah* to the girl. The Chafetz Chaim told the girl that if she would be careful not to speak any evil, she would live a long life.

All those who knew her avoided speaking *loshon hora* in her presence. If someone said anything resembling *loshon hora*, she would scold him as if her life depended on it. The girl lived for over one hundred and four years.

The great Rav Yisrael Abu Chatzeira was world-renowned for his ability to give successful *berachos*. Once, after he heard one of the leaders of the city speak *loshon hora*, he quickly moved away from that city. His extreme caution in his speech and even what he heard no doubt contributed to the effect of his words and his *berachos*.

Another example is recorded in the *Gemara*.[91] When Rav Yehoshua ben Levi was about to die, he jumped into Gan Eden and swore not to leave. Hashem said that since Rav Yehoshua had never sworn falsely and never profaned his speech, he did not need to leave.

The Chazon Ish had just finished saying his *Shabbos Tefillos* when a rich Sephardi Jew came running in to tell him that one of the water pipes in his house had burst. Water was flooding his house, damaging the rugs and expensive furniture.[92]

"Please, *Rebbe*, can I fix the pipe?" he begged. He was very disappointed when he received a negative reply.

"But water is running all over the house," the man persisted.

"The law cannot be changed because of this," the Chazon Ish answered.

The man persisted.

"What do you want me to do?" the Chazon Ish finally asked. "Tell it to stop?"

"Yes, please," the man begged.

"All right, stop!" the Chazon Ish ordered.

Sure enough, it stopped.

※※※※

Silent Blessing

Loshon hora is so powerful a tool that its absence brings blessings.

One tragedy after another happened in the Jewish community of Chicago.[93] Many families suffered losses due to accidents and sickness, and the entire community was distressed.

At last, one community-minded woman decided that something had to be done to protect the city. She emphasized the concept of not speaking *loshon hora* in the schools and also stressed the importance of adult education in the matter.

Soon, three cancer cases in the community were cured. In the summer, the woman brought her project to the area where she was staying in the mountains, and in comparison to previous summers, there was an unexplainable nearly 100% decrease in accidents.

Not speaking *loshon hora* is even good for the teeth.[94] The great Rabbi Horowitz lived over a hundred years with a perfect set of teeth. This was before modern dentistry, when almost all elderly people had rotted teeth.

When Rabbi Horowitz was *Bar Mitzvah*, he ended his *drashah* with a public resolution not to speak any *loshon hora*. Those who knew him could testify that he kept his resolution faithfully. The strongest testimony came from his own mouth, by the condition of his teeth.

꙳꙳꙳꙳

When to Listen

In this *Parshah* we find that Yaakov was about to disclose to his sons exactly when *Mashiach* would come. At the last moment, the *Shechinah* left him, as a sign that he was not permitted to disclose this secret. And so the timing of *Mashiach's* arrival remains a mystery.

However, Yaakov did give a hint. He told his sons, "Gather together to listen to my words." This was a hint that when the Jewish people unite and have no hatred among themselves, *Mashiach* will come.

The *Gemara*[95] states that the *Bais Hamikdash* was destroyed because of *loshon hora* and needless hatred. When we mend this sin, we can joyfully await *Mashiach*. But even as we wait, we can enjoy the immediate blessings that guarding our tongues can bring.

There are times when we cannot remain silent but must speak or hear *loshon hora*. However, we must be careful not to overdo it. There are exceptional circumstances in which not listening to *loshon hora* can pose its threats. For this reason it is important to learn the laws of *loshon hora*.

After the first *Bais Hamikdash* was destroyed and most of the Jews were killed or exiled, the wicked king Nevuchadnezzar allowed only the poor, weak Jews to remain in Eretz Yisrael to keep the land from becoming barren. He appointed Gedaliah as the leader over the remaining few Jews.₉₆ Gedaliah, a *tzaddik*, began restoring and strengthening the remnants of our people, and in the course of time, rebuilt a proud and prosperous nation. Since he was loyal to Nevuchadnezzar, Gedaliah did not bear any opposition from him.

However, there were Jews who were disloyal to Nevuchadnezzar. They felt strong enough to overthrow his rule. Yishmael ben Nesanya, a secret opponent of Gedaliah, had planned to kill Gedaliah and start a rebellion. The King of Amon offered to aid him in the rebellion.

Gedaliah's friend, Yochanan ben Karayach, was aware of the secret conspiracy between the King of Amon and Yishmael. He warned Gedaliah that Yishmael was planning to kill him and asked Gedaliah for permission to kill Yishmael secretly. Gedaliah did not believe the evil reports about Yishmael and would not give permission to have him killed. While Gedaliah was right in that an evil report is not sufficient evidence to kill someone, he acted unwisely by taking no precautions whatsoever.

When Yishmael came with his men, Gedaliah ate alone with them, with no guards present. Yishmael and his men took advantage of this opportunity and killed Gedaliah.

When the Jews heard about this, they panicked and fled

to Egypt. Gedaliah's assassination destroyed all hope of rebuilding Eretz Yisrael and set off a chain of disasters. Gedaliah is held responsible for all the evil that resulted because he failed to properly take heed of beneficial *loshon hora*.

The *Gemara* tells us that, although Gedaliah was correct for not believing entirely what was said, he was wrong for completely ignoring it.[98] If one hears something that may be detrimental, one must be cautious.

At the same time, however, we cannot hurt others in any way because of mere hearsay. We certainly cannot spread such rumors or believe them, as the following episode demonstrates:[98]

There was once a rumor that two Jews were guilty of killing someone. When the Roman government began to chase them, they came to Rav Tarfon and begged him to hide them out, for they claimed they were really innocent.

"I cannot hide you," said Rav Tarfon. "For I must take into consideration that there may be some truth to the rumor, and if so, the Romans will kill me after they investigate. Go and hide yourselves."

From here, we derive that one can be wary of rumors and take the proper precautions.[99] Still, Rav Tarfon ordered them to hide, for he did not believe they were murderers.

In certain situations, it is necessary to speak *loshon hora* However, caution must be exercised. One must ascertain that no alternative exists and that the information is correct. One may not exaggerate or give the impression that things are worse than they actually are. Also, other conditions must be met as explained in the *Chafetz Chaim.*[100] When something must be said, one must not remain silent. Don't make Gedaliah's mistake and go too far by dismissing everything and not taking heed. The calamity that can result could affect *Klal Yisrael* for generations to come.

༈༈༈

They Had Good Intentions

Speaking *loshon hora*, even for beneficial purposes, is like playing with fire. One must be careful. Reuven, Shimon and Levi meant well but were careless in defining the honor of their family. The results of their actions flawed their own characters. Yaakov gave them a rebuke instead of a blessing.

Character is affected by outward actions.[101] It is told that a king took a ruthless criminal and made him headmaster of an orphanage. After a few years, he stopped being so ruthless. Being forced to perform acts of kindness had an effect on him. When the king made a kind man become an executioner, it had the opposite effect.

If one defames and belittles another person, even when necessary, it may ruin one's own character.

R av Moshe Chaim Luzzato, author of the *Mesillas Yesharim*, was a child prodigy, the delight of his great teacher Rabbi Yishay Bassan, author of *Lachmei Todah*. At the age of fourteen, he was well versed in the entire *Talmud*. At seventeen, he published the book *Leshon Limudim*, which was praised by the Torah leaders of that time. At the age of twenty, he had reached such perfection that an angel descended from heaven each day to teach him the hidden secrets of the Torah. Eliyahu Hanavi also came to him on a regular basis. Rav Luzzato wrote many books based on what he learned from the angel and from Eliyahu, but he did not publish these works. They were studied only by a select group of disciples.

For three years, he taught his disciples without any disturbances. Once, Rav Luzzato needed to go to another city. While he was away, a scholar from Eretz Yisrael came for a visit and befriended Rav Luzzato's students. They told him about the greatness of their rabbi and revealed to him the secret commentaries he had written. The visitor was overwhelmed and wrote letters to his friends describing this amazing *Talmid Chacham*. He disclosed the fact that the commentaries were explanations revealed by angels and Eliyahu Hanavi.

Many people were apprehensive when they heard such a description given to any person, for it was only a short time after the era of Shabbesai Tzvi, the infamous false *Mashiach*, who had been a source of strife for the Jews.

The claim that the young Rabbi Luzzato attained such high spiritual levels aroused much suspicion. It was not conceivable that anyone in that generation should be visited regularly by Eliyahu Hanavi and an angel, and certainly not at such a young age. There was concern that he would also pose a threat to the Jews.

There were those who decided that his influence must be halted immediately and permanently. To accomplish this, they wrote letters to the leaders of the surrounding communities denouncing him in strong terms. Rav Bassan, his teacher, tried to defend him and prove that any accusations against him were false, but to no avail.

Rav Bassan saw how persistent the opposition was. To bring peace and save Rav Luzzato's reputation, Rav Bassan asked Rav Luzzato to surrender all his works to him and to sign an agreement that he would no longer write books that dealt with mystical interpretations without Rav Bassan's consent. Rav Luzzato understandably consented. Things quieted down for some time, until it was once again rumored that Rabbi Luzzato was not keeping his agreement and was writing mystical works. When Rabbi Luzzato saw there was no end to the false rumors fabricated against him and that the strife would not end, he decided to leave Italy.

Leaving his wife and child behind, he went to Amsterdam. Rabbi Luzzato traveled with a heavy heart. Circumstances had forced him to leave not only his family but also his disciples. He was forced to give up all that was precious to him in life because of false accusations.

In Germany, he had to travel through the city of Frankfurt, whose community had been given a vivid description of how dangerous he was. In Frankfurt, he was seized and locked up in a room. His only chance for freedom was to sign a confession stating that he had attempted to deceive others about his greatness, and in truth, it was all a bluff. This confession was copied and widely distributed, causing him much disgrace.

Rabbi Luzzato finally reached Amsterdam, and to his surprise, the people in Amsterdam received him with much respect. One of the wealthier men gave him a place to stay and provided him with all his needs. Any letters that were received disgracing Rabbi Luzzato were completely ignored. Finally, he could again share his Torah knowledge with the many scholars who came to him.

It was here in Amsterdam that he wrote, with his teacher's consent, the famous *Mesillas Yesharim*. Any Torah leader will testify that whoever has been influenced by this masterpiece is truly fortunate.

ﭏ ﭏ ﭏ ﭏ

To Tell the Truth

After Yaakov passed away, Yosef and his brothers brought Yaakov to Eretz Yisrael for burial. Yosef interrupted his journey and visited Shechem to thank Hashem for miraculously saving him from the snakes and scorpions in the pit, which was located in Shechem. [103] The brothers misunderstood Yosef's intentions and read Yosef's stopover in Shechem as an indication that he intended to take revenge against them for throwing him into the pit.

In fear of Yosef, they said that Yaakov had requested that Yosef forgive them and not take revenge. Yaakov had never even been told about the whole incident. However, they felt that fabricating this story was the only way to make peace with him. They knew Yosef would fulfill his father's wishes. This fabrication caused Yosef great pain, because it showed that his brothers suspected him of bad feelings and arrogance.

110

The Chafetz Chaim writes that if one is asked a question and a truthful answer will cause hatred or *loshon hora*, one should avoid answering the question. [104] However, if one has no choice, or if being silent in itself will give a negative impression, it is best to answer untruthfully.

When Yaakov blessed his son Asher, he said, "Asher's land will be fertile, and its produce will be used to give delicacies for the king."

In Hebrew, delicacies for the king are called *ma'adanei melech*. This brings to mind a tragic and true story about the author of the *sefer* called *Ma'adanei Melech*, and how this title was used against him in order to embitter his life.

R abbi Yom Tov Lippmann Heller, the author of *Ma'adanei Melech*, was world renowned for the *Tosefos Yom Tov*, his commentary on *Mishnayos*. His interpretations were so widely accepted that there is hardly a *Mishnayos* printed in the last few hundred years without his commentary on the same page.

Rabbi Heller was the rabbi of Prague for twenty-eight years. However, he did not need the rabbinate for support, as he was not only wise but wealthy. He was the *Av Bais Din* (head of the Rabbinical court) and presided whenever there were disputes. He always meted out fair judgment according to the Torah, regardless of the prestige and position of the litigants.

Once, he ruled against a prestigious, wealthy man by the name of Menashe Steinhart who in his anger subsequently conceived a plot to remove Rabbi Yom Tov from the rabbinate. [105] This was no simple task, since Rabbi Yom Tov was well loved and accepted by his entire community.

Menashe was extremely wealthy. Many princes borrowed great sums of money from him, and he was extremely influential in the government. He persuaded some government officials to aid him in slandering Rabbi Yom Tov to the Emperor, claiming that although his *sefer* was called *Delicacies of the King*, it really disparaged the king and his religion. Menashe had only intended to have Rabbi Yom Tov removed from his position, but as with all *loshon hora*, there is no telling to what calamity it can lead.

The Emperor ordered that Rabbi Yom Tov be imprisoned. He was put on trial and faced a possible death sentence for treason. The community of Prague was in an uproar. Moreover, not only was the life of Rabbi Yom Tov in danger, but plans were being made to expel the entire community. History has proven that expelling people from their homes and condemning them to wander is tantamount to manslaughter through hunger and starvation.

Rabbi Yom Tov's life and the community were miraculously saved, nevertheless.

Rabbi Yom Tov's oldest son Shmuel had been learning in a *Yeshiva* in Metz, France. Summoned by his father, he set out for Prague on one of his periodic visits.

As Shmuel passed through the wilderness he heard voices shouting, "Help! Help! Save us!" He saw a wild bull running after a noblewoman, her small boy and their maid. The animal had been enraged by the maid's red kerchief. Shmuel ran to the maid, removed the kerchief from her head and threw it at the feet of the animal, who dashed forward and attacked it with its horns. Meanwhile, the woman and her child hid behind the trees.

Precisely at that moment, a carriage drew up with a

nobleman in it. It was none other than the noblewoman's husband, the French ambassador. The noblewoman told her husband what had transpired and how Shmuel had saved their lives. The Ambassador offered Shmuel a large reward, but Shmuel declined. His only wish was that the ambassador remember that he was a Jew and that the people of the Jewish nation were his friends.

When Shmuel returned home and learned of his father's imprisonment, he eventually turned to the ambassador for aid. The ambassador promised he would do everything in his power.

Due to the ambassador's influence, Rabbi Yom Tov's life was spared. However, he was not permitted to remain in a rabbinical position and was fined with an enormous fine, payable in installments. Rabbi Yom Tov was forced to sell all he owned and was driven into extreme poverty for many years. Since he was only suited for the rabbinate, he was deprived of a means to support his family. Any money he managed to earn had to be used for paying the fine.

This terrible situation lasted for three long years, until a group of his close friends raised money for the last installment.

When Menashe, the main instigator of the plot, lay on his deathbed, he sent for Rabbi Yom Tov. He confessed that he was the cause of all Rabbi Yom Tov's misery and was very aggrieved over all he had done. He had been dissatisfied with the Rav's decision against him, and he had only wanted him to lose his position as Chief of the Jewish Court. This certainly was a great sin, and he had had no idea of the consequences of his plot. He begged that the *Rav* forgive him and pray that his life be spared.

Rabbi Yom Tov wholeheartedly consented to pray for him, and Menashe recovered. Many years after Menashe died, Rabbi Yom Tov recorded the story without mentioning any names. Rabbi Yom Tov commanded all his descendants to commemorate the day he was arrested, the fifth day of *Tamuz*, as a day of fasting and repenting.

꾸꾸꾸꾸

Sharing Your Secret

The *Parshah* concludes with the burial of Yaakov. Yaakov did not disclose the time of *Mashiach's* arrival to his sons. This remained a secret shared only by Hashem and Yaakov.

Nothing strengthens a relationship between two parties as much as having a mutual secret. Each party feels secure and confident in the other. The longer the secret is kept, the richer the relationship becomes.

When you know *loshon hora* about someone and you restrain yourself from saying it, only Hashem shares your secret, and you feel His confidence in you that you won't disclose it.

Nothing can bring one closer to Hashem, may His Name be blessed.

GLOSSARY

FOOTNOTES

DEDICATION

GLOSSARY

Aveirah: sin

Avodah Zarah: idol worship

Bachur: Yeshiva student

Bachurim: Yeshiva students

Bais Hamedrash: Hall of Torah study

Bais Hamikdash: Temple in Jerusalem

Bar Mitzvah: ceremony for males at 13, the age at which they are obligated to keep all the Torah's commandments

Ben: the son of

Berachah: blessing

Berachos: plural of blessing

Bnai Yisrael: Jews

Canaan: the land of Israel; the grandson of Noach and the nation descending from him

Chachamim: Torah sages

Chassan: groom

Chassidic: pertaining to *Chassidim*

Chassidim: Jews who follow the customs and teachings of Rav Yisrael Baal Shem Tov

Chazal: our Rabbis of blessed memory

Chazarah: review

Cheishek: desire

Chillul Hashem: desecration of the Name

Duchen: pronounce the blessing of the *Kohanim*

Eretz Yisrael: the land of Israel

Erev Shabbos: day preceding the *Shabbos*

Gemara: the *Talmud*

Halacha: Jewish law

Halachic: pertaining to Jewish law

Hamotzi: benediction on bread

Hanavi: the prophet

Havdalah: prayer recited over wine at closing of *Shabbos* and Holidays

Kaddish: prayer in merit of the deceased

Kallah: bride

Kashrus: kosher status

Kiddush: blessings on wine before *Shabbos* and holiday meals

Kohain: descendant of Aharon who serves in the *Bais Hamikdash*

Kohain Gadol: the highest ranking *Kohain* (descendant of Aharon, who officiated in the *Bais Hamikdash*)

Kohanim: plural of *Kohain*

Kollel: group of *Yeshiva* students who study Torah after marriage

Loshon Hora: evil speech

Machzor: prayerbook for holidays

Malachim: angels

Mashgiach: supervisor

Mashiach: Messiah

Meforshim: commentaries

Midrash: commentary on the Torah, compiled by sages of the *Talmud*

Mishnah: unit of *Mishnayos*

Mishnayos: sections of the Oral law compiled by Rav Yehuda Hanassi

Misnagdim: antagonists of the *Chassidim* who instead followed the teachings of the Vilna Gaon

Mitzva: Torah commandment, good deed

Mitzvos: plural of *Mitzvah*

Motzai Shabbos: Saturday night

Niftar: died

Olam Habo: the world to come

Parshah: chapter in the Torah

Payit: additional prayers customary for the Holidays

Poretz: landowner

Rashi: commentary on *Chumash, Tanach* and *Gemara*

Rav: Rabbi

Rebbe: Jewish teacher; Rabbi

Rechilus: statements which cause hatred between people

Resha'im: wicked people

Rosh Yeshivah: dean of a Yeshiva

Rov: Rabbi

Satan: evil angel

Seder: special feast on Passover

Sefarim: Hebrew books

Sefer: Hebrew book

Shabbos: Sabbath

Shadchan: matchmaker

Shechinah: Divine Presence

Shidduch: match

Shiurim: Talmudical discourses

Shofar: ram's horn

Shul: synagogue

Shulchan Aruch: Code of Jewish Law

Shvatim: the sons of Yaakov; the twelve tribes

Simanim: codes

Simchas Torah: festival observed the day after *Sukkos*

Sukkos: Holiday of Tabernacles

Talmid Chacham: Torah scholar

Talmidei Chachamim: Torah scholars

Talmidim: pupils

Talmud: Oral Law

Tanach: Books of the Prophets

Tefillos: prayers

Tehillim: Psalms

Tenaim: engagement agreement

Teshuvah: repentance

Tosfos: early commentary on the Talmud

Tzaddik: righteous man

Tzaddikim: righteous people

Tzadeykes: righteous woman

Tzedakah: charity

Yahrzeit: anniversary of one's death

Yasher Koach: praise for a job well done

Yeshiva: Academy of Torah learning

Yeshivos: plural of Yeshiva

Yetzer Hora: evil inclination

Yom Tov: Holiday

Yovail: fifty-year cycle

Footnotes and Sources

1. *Shmiras Haloshon*, Vol. 2 Ch. 1
2. *Ibid.*
3. True story adapted (with permission) from the book *Horishon Leshalsheles Brisk* by Rabbi Chaim Karlinski of New York
4. *Arachin* 15b
5. *Beraishis* 11:28
6. Rambam, *Hilchos Dayos* 7:5
7. *Bava Basra* 22a
8. *Shabbos* 149b
9. *Sanhedrin* 95a
10. True story adapted (with permission) from the book *Horishon Leshalsheles Brisk.*
11. *Beraishis* 11:32
12. Rashi, *Beraishis* 17:5
13. Rashi, *Devarim* 2:5
14. Rashi, *Beraishis* 29:19
15. Told by Rabbi Noson Wachtfogel, Mashgiach of Lakewood Yeshiva
16. Rashi, *Beraishis* 18:13
17. *Chafetz Chaim*, Laws of *Rechilus* 8:4 and footnote 6
18. *Chafetz Chaim*, Laws of *Rechilus* 1:8
19. *Chafetz Chaim*, Laws of *Loshon Hora* 4:10
20. Rashi, *Beraishis* 19:4
21. *Chafetz Chaim*, Laws of *Loshon Hora* 10:2
22. Rashi, *Beraishis* 18:21
23. *Chafetz Chaim*, Laws of *Loshon Hora* 10:13
24. Rashi, *Beraishis* 19:37
25. Told by Rabbi Sholom Shvadron *shlita* and Rabbi Yaakov Kamenetzky *zatzal*
26. Rashi, *Beraishis* 24:39
27. *Beraishis*, 9:22-25
28. *Sanhedrin* 39: This story does not appear in the standard text but in the text of the Geonim. See *Chachmah Umussar* from Rabbi Simcha Zisel Ziv
29. Told by Rabbi Isaac Ausband, Rosh Yeshivah of Telshe
30. Preface to the *Sefer Chafetz Chaim*
31. Reprinted (with permission) from Ron's *New World*
32. The Tzaddik Reb Nachumke
33. See ArtScroll's Reb Nachumke for detailed story
34. *Bava Basra* 109
35. *Be'er Mayim Chaim* 1:15 and 2:28 and *Chafetz Chaim* 7:6
36. There are numerous versions of this story amongst the various biographies of the Chafetz Chaim.
37. *Beraishis* 27:36
38. *Chafetz Chaim*, Laws of *Rechilus* 9:2-3
39. Rashi, *Beraishis* 26:13

40. *Chafetz Chaim*, Laws of *Loshon Hora* 10:2
41. Rashi, *Beraishis* 27:46
42. *Beraishis Rabba* 70:4
43. *Shmiras Halashon*, Vol. 2, Ch. 10
44. Story retold by subject
45. Rashi, *Beraishis* 30:22
46. Story retold by subject
47. *Tehillim* 34:13
48. Story told by subject
49. *Pe'ah* 8:9
50. *Akeidas Yitzchak, Parshas Vayetze*
51. *Ibid.*
52. *Ohr Hachaim, Beraishis* 31:36
53. Told by Reb Koppel
54. *Zohar, Beraishis* 167b
55. *Beraishis Rabba* 78:18, quoted in *Ramban* 33:15
56. *Chafetz Chaim*, Laws of *Loshon Hora* Ch. 10
57. Heard from various sources
58. Story brought in numerous biographies of Chafetz Chaim
59. *Shmuel I*, Ch. 2
60. *Rosh Hashanah* 18a
61. *Tehillim* 34:13
62. A story told by the Klausenberger Rav, quoted in the biography of the Chasam Sofer
63. *Orach Chaim* 271:12
64. *Sefer Sipurei Hachassidim* by Rabbi Yosaif Zevin
65. *Shmiras Halashon*, Vol. 2, Ch. 11
66. Rashi, *Beraishis* 40:1
67. *Payit* for *Yom Kippur Mussaf* entitled *Ayleh Ezkerah*, These I Remember
68. *Kovetz Ma'amarim* by Rabbi Elchanan Wasserman
69. *Beraishis* 37:15
70. Told by the Rabbi's student
71. Parable from common experience
72. *Kiddushin* 70a
73. *Vayikra* 25:9
74. *Chinuch, Mitzvah* 331
75. *Sforno, Beraishis* 37:2
76. *Chafetz Chaim*, Chapter 4:4
77. Famous parable
78. Rashi, *Beraishis* 41:12
79. *Yevamos* 63
80. *Shmiras Halashon*, Vol. 2 Ch. 12
81. Rashi, *Beraishis* 42:27
82. *Orchos Tzadikkim* Ch. 25 quoted from *Yalkut Tehillim* 521 and *Shochar Tov* 39:2. This English version is adapted from the works of Chaya M. Cohen, Israel.

83. *Chafetz Chaim*, Laws of *Loshon Hora* 3:1
84. *Beraishis* 42:1
85. *Shmiras Halashon*, Ch. 6
86. Based on *Chut Hameshulash*
87. *Shmiras Halashon*, Vol. 2, Ch. 11
88. *Shmiras Halashon*, Vol. 2, Ch. 12, end of *Parshas Vayaishev*
89. Retold by subject
90. *Baba Sali*, Hebrew edition, p. 65
91. *Kesuvos* 77a
92. Told by Rabbi Sholom Shvardron *shlita*
93. Witnessed by many members of the Chicago community
94. Told by Rabbi Horowitz's relatives
95. *Yoma* 9b
96. *Yirmiyahu*, Ch. 40
97. *Niddah* 61a
98. *Ibid.*
99. *Chafetz Chaim*, Laws of *Loshon Hora* 6:10
100. *Chafetz Chaim*, Laws of *Rechilus* 9
101. *Chinuch, Mitzvah* 16
102. Based on *Vayorem Moshe*
103. *Da'as Zekeinim, Beraishis* 50:16
104. *Chafetz Chaim*, Laws of *Rechilus* 1:8
105. Based on *Megillas Aiva*, translated and reprinted with permission from the English edition, entitled *The Fast and the Feast*.

This book is dedicated

In Memory of

Rebbetzin Frieda K. Hirmes ע״ה

by her children
and grandchildren

לז״נ ברוך משולם לבוביץ

Bernat Lebovitz

מאת משפחתו

לז״נ חיה חנה בת ר׳ חיים

Carrie Ann Kass

IN HONOR OF

Rabbi and Mrs. Laibel Shugerman
for their devotion to Torah ideals

Dr. Marcel Reisher

Rabbi & Mrs. A. Gottdiner

Mr. & Mrs. Bernard Steinharter

Mrs. Hannah Storch

Mr. & Mrs. Asher Bamberger